Manual for

Using the MMPI-2 as a
Therapeutic Intervention

D1015204

Manual for

Using the MMPI-2 as a Therapeutic Intervention

Stephen E. Finn

University of Minnesota Press
Minneapolis

Published by the University of Minnesota Press
111 Third Avenue South, Suite 290, Minneapolis, MN 55401-2520
Printed in the United States of America on acid-free paper

CIP data available. ISBN 0-8166-2885-8

Contents

Tables & Figures

Acknowledgments

I am deeply indebted to Mary E. Tonsager, who helped develop the intervention described in this manual and who conducted the initial research project that proved its effectiveness. Arnold H. Buss and Constance T. Fischer made extensive, helpful comments on an earlier draft of the manuscript. James Butcher, Alex Caldwell, Roger Greene, and David Nichols also provided useful suggestions.

The MMPI-2 as a Therapeutic Intervention

This manual describes an assessment procedure that uses the Minnesota Multiphasic Personality Inventory-2 (MMPI-2) with clients who are self-referred or referred by another mental-health professional for testing. The goal is to gather accurate information about clients with the MMPI-2 and then use this information to help clients understand themselves and make positive changes in their lives. When this procedure was used with college students awaiting psychotherapy, the students reported decreased symptomatology and increased self-esteem which persisted over a two-week follow-up (Finn and Tonsager, 1992).

The flow chart in Figure 1 outlines the major steps in the MMPI-2 intervention procedure, which requires approximately 90-120 minutes of client contact and an additional 30-60 minutes of the assessor's time apart from the client.

Assessors must be trained to use the intervention, and there is a great deal of art involved, which assessors develop by using the intervention repeatedly over time. However, one need not have extensive prior clinical training to use this intervention. For example, second-year clinical psychology graduate students working under supervision have been able to effectively use the intervention procedure after 8-10 hours of training.

If you are teaching yourself to do this intervention, I recommend that you read the entire manual quickly to get a sense of the complete intervention. Then read it again slowly, taking detailed notes on each specific step. (Tables 1 and 7 outline the steps in the initial interview and the feedback session.) As you will see, each step of the procedure is conceptually simple, but there are a number of fine points that require study and practice. After a careful reading, you may wish to try an MMPI-2 assessment with a client, using the manual as a guide and videotaping yourself so that you can do a self-critique afterward. Or you and several colleagues may study the manual, assess separate clients, and watch each other's videotapes. After 6-7 monitored assessments, most experienced assessors feel comfortable proceeding on their own, with occasional consultation.

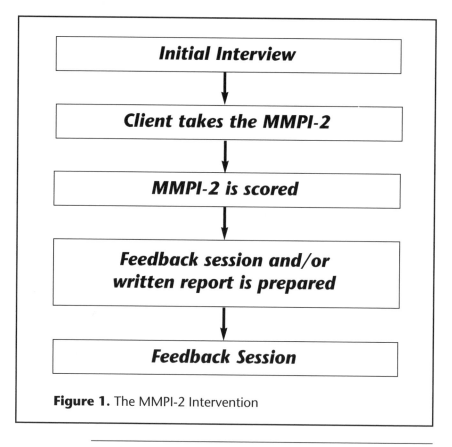

Figure 1. The MMPI-2 Intervention

Of course, as with all complex skills, initially you will probably feel that you are going by the numbers when you conduct an MMPI-2 intervention. Don't worry; this feeling goes away with practice, as you invest the intervention procedures with your own clinical style.[1]

General Principles Underlying the Intervention

The principles underlying the MMPI-2 intervention are:

1. Taking the MMPI-2 can be an unsettling experience for clients. It involves giving personal information of uncertain significance to an assessor (typically a stranger) who will use it to draw conclusions that could result in either help or harm to the client.

2. Clients should be tested with the MMPI-2 only when they fully understand the kind of information that can be derived from it and how that information will be used.

3. The assessor (the person administering and interpreting the MMPI-2) is ultimately responsible for clarifying with the client the goals and purpose of the MMPI-2 assessment.

4. Clients become most engaged in taking the MMPI-2 when they are treated as collaborators, whose ideas and cooperation are essential to the assessment.

5. Clients become most invested in an MMPI-2 assessment when the results will be used to address their personal goals.

6. When an MMPI-2 assessment addresses clients' goals and clients are treated as collaborators, they are more likely to give accurate and useful information when completing the test.

7. When clients understand the nature of an MMPI-2 assessment and freely agree to participate, they often look for

---

[1] Although the intervention described in this manual uses the MMPI-2, the general method and principles may be applied (with modifications) to other tests–or a battery of tests–as well.

emotional support and for new information that will help them address life problems.

8. Giving clients feedback about their MMPI-2 test results can help them understand and manage life problems.

9. When MMPI-2 feedback is given to clients in an emotionally supportive manner, they often feel affirmed, less anxious, and more hopeful, even if the test feedback seems likely to produce painful emotional reactions.

The above principles are discussed in Butcher and Finn (1983), Butcher (1990), Finn and Butcher (1991), Finn and Tonsager (1992), and Finn and Tonsager (in preparation). The intervention procedure described here is based largely on Fischer's (1985) model of collaborative assessment.

Step 1. The Initial Interview

Purpose

During the initial interview, the assessor meets with the client for 30-60 minutes. The goals of this initial meeting are to:

➤ Build rapport with the client

➤ Frame the assessment as a collaborative task

➤ Identify personal questions the client would like to have answered from the MMPI-2 results

➤ Collect background information relevant to the client's questions

➤ Inquire about past assessment experiences and show understanding for any past hurts

➤ Give the client permission to ask questions about the assessor

➤ Answer the client's questions and concerns about the assessment

➤ Arrange for the client to take the MMPI-2

➤   Decide when the feedback session will take place,
     where it will be conducted, and who will be present

➤   Introduce the MMPI-2 to the client

Building Rapport

Rapport between assessor and client is an essential compo-
nent of the MMPI-2 intervention, as it is with all therapies.
Early in the initial interview, rapport is aided by the assessor's
awareness of clients' anxiety and her/his ability to set clients
at ease. In my very first moments of contact with clients I give
forth a warm, reassuring presence. I greet clients with an
open smile, shake hands as I introduce myself, and then
direct them into my office while inviting them to sit where
they please. I then make a bit of small talk—asking if they
had difficulty finding my office or commenting on the weath-
er. After this, I pick up my clipboard and settle into my chair,
signaling that I am ready to get to work. I then look directly
at the client and say something like:

> *"Today we're going to meet for about 30 minutes to talk
> about the personality assessment you were interested in
> (or—that Dr. Smith asked you to do with me.) I see
> myself as a consultant to you (and Dr. Smith) to help you
> better understand what your situation is now. Therefore,
> today I'd like us to figure out what questions you'd like to
> have answered from the assessment. Then we'll use the
> testing to help you answer those questions. Today, I'll also
> be asking you about yourself so I can understand your
> assessment questions, and I'll answer any questions you
> have about me, the testing, or the feedback session that
> we'll have at the end of the assessment. Okay?"*

Notice how this introduction immediately communicates to
clients that the assessment is a collaborative enterprise: Their
input will be sought, they will receive feedback about the testing, and they will also have the opportunity to ask me ques-

tions. Even the interview will not be totally one-sided. By establishing the purpose of the initial meeting, I also show that I am a responsible expert, that I know my job, and that I won't be counting on them to do my work for me. I state the limits of my role: I am a consultant to them (and the referring professional) whose task it is to help them meet their goals. However, I also indicate my willingness to help clients determine what realistic questions for the assessment might be. After my brief introduction, I respond to any questions clients have at that point, then immediately proceed to the major work of the initial interview: framing the clients' questions for the assessment.

In the remainder of the initial interview, rapport is best served when the assessor communicates genuine interest and concern for the client. As I listen attentively and occasionally nod or comment, clients sense that I view them as people, not just as objects for observation. I pause here and there as I collect information to reflect back how much clients have been struggling, or how well they have handled a difficult situation. Such comments are not artificially calculated to build trust; rather, I share a few of my genuine reactions as I listen to clients' stories. Finally, as clients begin to experience their own impact on the assessment process (e.g., that they can decline to participate, specify what they want to learn, and have some say about when they will be tested), they typically feel less vulnerable and more trusting of me.

Framing the Client's Questions

This part of the initial interview can be tricky, because some allied professionals say almost nothing to clients before referring them for testing.[2] Nevertheless, I begin by directly asking, *"What would you like to learn about yourself from this assessment?"*

Some clients have well-articulated questions that they offer at this point: "My mother was schizophrenic and I want to

---

[2] I always ask referring professionals to discuss their goals for an assessment with clients and if possible to share with the clients the explicit questions they are asking me to address. Referring professionals can also assist clients before the initial interview to come up with the clients' questions for the assessment.

know if I have any signs of it myself," "My therapist says I am depressed and that this test will show how depressed I am," "I want to know what I'm so angry about all the time." Others will draw a complete blank, saying that they did not know I would be asking them this and have no idea what they want from the assessment. This response is usually an initial anxiety reaction that I meet with reassurance (e.g., "Of course you didn't know about this part of the assessment"), explanation (e.g., "I am interested in using tests to help people learn about themselves and thus it is very important for me to know what you would like to know from the testing"), and an offer of support (e.g., "Let's see if we can come up with some questions by talking together.") Following are frequent reactions and my responses:

Client: *"I have no idea. Dr. Smith just asked me to take the test. I don't have any reasons for taking it myself."*

Assessor: (If I know something about the presenting issue) *"Dr. Smith told me that you were having some problems with _____. Is there anything you'd like to know that might help you with that?"*

or

Assessor: *"What is your understanding of why Dr. Smith wanted you to do the assessment?"* (See if the client can identify Dr. Smith's questions.) *Are those questions you are interested in too?"*

∽∽ ∽∽ ∽∽

Client: *"I don't know. What kinds of things can the test tell me?"*

Assessor: *"Actually it tells quite a few different things. Why don't you tell me what questions you're thinking of, and if they can't be answered by the test, I'll be sure to let you know."*

Notice how I resist accepting the idea that clients cannot come up with their own questions. Most clients are not used to being treated as collaborators by mental-health professionals and find the whole idea of actively participating in the assessment quite foreign. If the assessor persists in showing genuine interest in clients' goals for the assessment, usually clients will eventually be able to state those goals, albeit with some assistance:

Client: *"Well I have been wondering why I keep choosing such losers for girlfriends, but I imagine the test can't tell me anything about that."*

Assessor: *"It might be able to tell us something about that. What kind of bad experiences have you had with girlfriends?"*

捠 捠 捠

Client: *"I'm such a procrastinator. I'm going to lose my job soon if I don't figure out why I put things off for so long."*

Assessor: *"It sounds like one of your questions is 'Why do I procrastinate at work even though it threatens my job?' Is that right?"*

Client: *"Yes, that sounds like a good question. Can the test answer that?"*

If clients continue to have difficulty coming up with assessment questions, I usually ask them to tell me what problems brought them to the referring person (or to me, if they are self-referred). I then listen with my "third ear" to be alert to possible questions:

Client: *" . . . that was my third girlfriend—the same pattern all over again! I thought she walked on water. But six months into the relationship I find out she's a criminal and a druggie! Once again I fell for a real manipulator!"*

Assessor: *"That must have been upsetting. I wonder if one question you might pose for the assessment is, 'Why do I keep choosing girlfriends who are really manipulators, but who I at first think are wonderful?' "*

This latter question might seem too broad to be meaningfully addressed by the MMPI-2, but I would accept it nonetheless, knowing that the MMPI-2 would have something to say about this man's interpersonal style in close relationships. Contrast this question with others that have to be narrowed down before they can be accepted as guides for the assessment:

Client:　　"*I want to know how to be a better mother.*"

Assessor:　"*Where do you have difficulties as a mother?*"

Client:　　"*I'm afraid to discipline my children. I think that if I start, I'm going to beat them like my father did me.*"

Assessor:　"*What makes you think that you might beat them?*"

Client:　　"*The anger I feel inside. Sometimes I feel that I can't control it.*"

Assessor:　"*That must be scary. Perhaps you'd like to ask the test about your anger, and whether you really seem to be at risk of beating your children.*"

∽ ∽ ∽

Client:　　"*My friend said this test would tell me if I'm crazy.*"

Assessor:　"*So have you been wondering about that?*"

Client:　　"*Well not really—but sometimes . . . My husband keeps saying I'm a nutcase because I always worry that he's having an affair. I guess I am a bit distrustful of men, but aren't most women?*"

Assessor:　"*So are you wondering if your distrust of men is more than most women feel?*"

Client:　　"*Exactly.*"

Assessor:　"*Well that's a good question we can pose for the assessment. Can you tell me a bit more about your thoughts that your husband is having an affair?*"

Many clients will pose questions about the etiology or source of their problems in living. Such questions can almost always be reframed into requests for help:

Client: *"I want to know why I am afraid of getting close to women. Is it because of the way my mother treated me when I was young?"*

Assessor: *"Hmmm . . . What would that mean to you—if you knew that your fear of women was because of your mother?"*

Client: *"Well that would mean that I should talk more about my mother in therapy, right?"*

Assessor: *"I see, so basically you want to know what steps to take in getting over your fear of closeness with women?"*

Client: *"Yes, I guess that's the most important question. Let's use that."*

Assessor: *"Okay, good—because the test really won't be able to tell us much about your relationship with your mother."*

As assessment questions are formed, I record them verbatim and then read them back to clients for confirmation. If I haven't gotten an assessment question "just right," I encourage clients to modify it until they are comfortable with the wording and feel that the question reflects what they would like to know from the assessment:

Assessor: *"So it sounds like your question is 'Why don't I see problems in my marriage that my wife sees?' Is that right?"*

Client: *"Not quite. That makes it sound like the problems are there and I'm not sure that they are."*

Assessor: *"Can you help me word a question that seems right?"*

Client: *"How about: 'Why don't my wife and I agree about whether there are problems in our marriage?'"*

Assessor: *"That's a good question. It helps me realize, however, that we may need to do things a bit differently. Most of your questions are about your marriage, so I may not be able to answer them without also seeing your wife. Do you think she would be willing to participate in the assessment?"*

This latter example demonstrates that jointly framing assessment questions does more than ensure semantic agreement between the assessor and client. As the assessor and client work together to form questions, both become clearer about their expectations for the assessment, creating an assessment contract that goes beyond the sum of their individual agendas. Together, the assessor and client construct an "observation deck" on which both may stand during the assessment. This step enlists the client's cooperation and sets the stage for most clients to be quite open in responding to the MMPI-2. Last, as will be discussed later, the shared assessment questions create an opening for the assessor and client to explore test results during the feedback session.

Collecting Background Information

Typically, after several assessment questions are agreed upon, I begin to collect background information that will help me understand those questions: When did a problem begin? Are there situations in which it is more frequent or intense, less so, or totally absent? How has the client already tried to address the problem? Did the client's solution work, and if so why did the client stop using that solution? What are the client's hypotheses about the source and continuance of the problem? Does the client know anyone else who has had similar problems?

Notice that this goal-centered interview is quite different from the general diagnostic interview that is often conducted at the beginning of a traditional assessment. The goal-centered approach honors the evolving contract between client and assessor because the assessor typically asks only for information that is ostensibly related to the client's questions. This practice decreases clients' anxiety by demonstrating that the assessor is following their agenda for the assessment. At times, the assessor may seek information that appears unrelated to clients' assessment goals; however, the assessor should provide a rationale for the new line of inquiry and ask clients' permission to delve into this area:

Assessor: *"So you and your wife began to disagree more last year, after she went back to work?"*

Client: *"Yes, she says I don't respect her work and act like my career is more important than hers."*

Assessor: *"And do you mind if I ask—it might be important to what's been happening between you and your wife— how has your own work been going?"*

Client: *"Actually—I don't know if it's related or not—but right after my wife went back to work we had a number of financial crises in my company. In fact, I almost went bankrupt last year."*

Assessor: *"I'm sorry. Has that made things very difficult for you?"*

To return to the earlier metaphor, the assessor and client have constructed an observation deck over a certain area of the client's life. If the assessor wants to expand the observation deck to take in an additional view, she/he proposes the change to the client and explains how the new addition may benefit the client. The client can then become more relaxed with the assessor—knowing that the assessor will not stray into sensitive areas without first asking the client's permission.

Dealing with Clients' Reservations about Assessment

Sometimes, even after the assessor has explained the collaborative nature of the assessment, clients hold back in establishing joint goals for the assessment or in giving background information about a particular set of questions. When this occurs, a client most likely has reservations about the whole assessment process, and it is usually best to stop and deal with these before attempting to proceed with the initial interview.[3] Such misgivings may range from concerns about confidentiality (e.g., Who will have access to the test results?) or the purpose of the referral (e.g., Are the test results going to be used to blame the client for family or couple problems?) to other concerns unique to the client (e.g., a fear of being revealed as "a bad person" on the MMPI-2). Second thoughts may also emerge later in the interview, when the assessment contract is being formalized.

Whenever such concerns are voiced, or if I sense that they are impeding the interview, I inquire about clients' uncertainty before I make any move to proceed with the interview. Sometimes merely listening to and acknowledging clients' reservations is enough to allay them. For example, a client who is ambivalent about getting an answer to a question may be aided if I show empathy for this dilemma and help the client explore the costs and benefits of knowing or not knowing more about a particular difficulty. At other times, I find a way to address clients' apprehensions directly, in the contract for the assessment. For example, an adolescent boy may be worried that his parents will use assessment results as evidence that he is the sole problem in the family. Obviously, I cannot guarantee that his parents won't try to do this. However, I might promise the boy that I'll be looking at the whole family in attempting to understand his problems and share my firm belief that family problems are never one person's responsibility. I might also suggest that he and I discuss

---

[3] Involuntary assessments–where clients are referred against their will for testing (e.g., by the court, or for employment screening)–are not covered in this manual. They will be discussed in an upcoming book (Finn & Tonsager, in preparation).

the assessment results together before we talk with his parents, making it clear that I want his involvement when the results are presented to his parents.

Hurts from Past Assessments

There is one class of clients' misgivings that occurs quite frequently and that cannot be addressed simply by modifying the assessment contract: clients' hurt feelings from past assessment experiences. The most frequent complaints concern test feedback, e.g., that clients were not given feedback about test results, sometimes even after spending many hours taking part in a battery of psychological tests. Others received feedback in ways that felt abusive and humiliating to them, or found the test feedback largely incomprehensible because highly technical language was used.[4]

Additional common grievances fall in several areas:

Informed consent

➤ no one fully explained the purpose of the assessment and explicitly asked the client if she/he was willing to participate

➤ the client was depressed, psychotic, or otherwise unable to fully consent to the assessment

➤ undue pressure was brought on the client to participate in the assessment

Conduct of the assessment

➤ testing sessions were overly long and draining

➤ the assessor was cold and harsh during the testing sessions

---

[4] The latest set of *Ethical Principles of Psychologists* (APA, 1992) now specifies that all clients should be given feedback about test results in such a way that they can understand those results.

➤ the client was chastised during the testing for being defensive or uncooperative

➤ testing sessions stirred up disturbing feelings in the client for which no support was made available

Use of the assessment results

➤ test results were revealed to family without the client's consent

➤ the client did not realize that the assessment results would be widely available to all treatment staff in an inpatient setting

➤ results were used to justify treatments that the client experienced as abusive or punishing

Obviously, any of these experiences can affect the way clients approach a current assessment. Thus, it is important that assessors and clients talk about such hurts before clients are asked to take the MMPI-2. I feel there are five important steps assessors must take in such a dialogue:

1. Show genuine interest in hearing about the client's past experience with assessment, usually by asking encouraging questions. If I am taking notes, I often lay down my pad at this point to make sure the client knows I am listening carefully. I probe to assist the client in telling the full story of the past hurt. For example:

Client: *"Oh, the MMPI! I hate that test! They made me take it in the hospital."*

Assessor: *"What do you hate about it?"*

Client: *"It's so long. And I was so confused I could barely turn around. They kept pushing me to finish it—telling me I couldn't have visits from my family until it was done.*

> *And then they made me do it all over again, saying that
> I hadn't really read the questions!"*

Assessor: *"So how many times did you have to do it altogether?"*

2. Demonstrate empathy about the past hurt by making a
reflective statement that goes beyond the client's initial
recounting. For example, to continue the above dialogue:

Assessor: *"So you were confused and just trying to get your head
together and all the time they were pushing you to take
the MMPI?"*

Client: *"Yes, it was awful!"*

Assessor: *"I hear that, and it must have felt even worse that they
used visits with your family to try to hurry you up."*

Client: *"You're right. At first I didn't have anything against the
test, but after a while it felt like they were blackmailing
me to take it. And nobody ever told me why it was so
damn important in the first place!"*

Assessor: *"So all this pressure and blackmail, and nobody even
told you what the testing was about. Did that add to
your confusion?"*

I have found that the best way I can show clients that I understand such experiences is to give voice to their vulnerability in
the testing situation. This breeds trust in me also, by showing
that I am aware of this dimension of the assessment experience even if previous assessors were not:

Assessor: *"So there you were, already confused and having problems, and then being pressured to take a test that you
had never heard of and didn't understand. You really
didn't have much choice, did you?"*

Client: *"So that sounds pretty awful to you? It's not just me?"*

3. Clearly state that you feel that assessment procedures used in the past instance were inappropriate or ill-advised:

Assessor: *"I want you to know that I don't approve of the way*
            they pushed you to take the MMPI in the hospital. It
            seems to me that the test would have been a lot easier
            for you if they had waited a bit longer until you were
            less confused, or explained the test better to you. And I
            certainly think that it was wrong to use your family vis-
            its as an incentive to get you to finish the MMPI."

This step is essential to fully enlisting the client's cooperation in the assessment. When we as professionals are willing to take a client's side about the misuse of assessment, the client knows that we put respect and ethical conduct above any desire to protect our colleagues. Also, such statements signal that we will protect the client's rights and try to prevent abuses of power from occurring in the current assessment. In such a context, clients are able to be truly open during an assessment, which maximizes the chance of the assessment intervention having a profound therapeutic impact.[5]

4. Offer a contract in the current assessment that addresses the past hurtful circumstances.
If the client is upset about never having received test feedback, promise that feedback will be given. If confidentiality was breached, go over the rules of confidentiality that you will be following. If testing sessions were long and grueling, promise rest breaks and urge the client to inform you when a break is needed.

---

[5] Of course, the assessor must remember that clients may misunderstand or misreport elements of the previous assessment situation. If a clear ethical violation has occurred, the assessor must alert clients of their rights, involve the referring professionals, and follow the rules and statutes that apply in reporting such situations.

Sometimes a client will continue to complain about an aspect of assessment that cannot be modified without drastically interfering with the goals of the assessment. If the assessment cannot be conducted without this element, I say so, and always give the client the option of not participating in the assessment. For example, adolescents may grumble that the MMPI-A is "boring." This complaint can be a sign of their anxiety about the test, but it also clearly reflects reality. I can acknowledge the tedium of completing a long True-False personality inventory, suggest that breaks be taken during the testing, require only the first 350 items to be completed, and perhaps even offer a computer-assisted administration (which is often more interesting to adolescents). However, I cannot get around the length of the MMPI-A. If the adolescent then decides not to participate in the assessment, I must—in the collaborative model—accept this decision gracefully.

Sometimes it is only at such a point—when the assessor demonstrates a true willingness to forgo the assessment rather than attempt to coerce the client—that a client's trust of the assessor is born. By being ready to face the difficulties entailed in not doing the assessment (including dealing with referring professionals) the assessor convincingly demonstrates that she/he is primarily concerned about the client's feelings. This type of situation is all too rare to clients who have felt abused by previous assessors.

5. Ask to be alerted if the client feels mistreated at any point during the assessment. This step communicates that although you will be attentive to the client's safety, you also count on the client to be responsible for her/his own well-being. Such an expectation shows respect for the client's competence and further demonstrates that you are not putting the client in a helpless role.

Restating the Assessment Questions

When past hurts have been addressed and clients' questions have been framed, I read aloud the entire list of assessment questions and once again ask clients to check their wording and accuracy. After any modifications are made, I encourage clients to let me know, at any point in the assessment, if further questions arise. I also repeat that I will do my best to answer these questions from their test results.

Encouraging the Client to Ask Questions of the Assessor

The traditional initial interview format, in which assessors ask all the questions and clients give all the answers, encourages clients to view themselves as passive participants who are being "acted upon." Yet another way that I challenge such a view is to encourage clients to ask me questions in the initial interview, before the assessment contract is finalized. Here's an excerpt from a recent assessment[6] :

SF: *"Well those are the assessment questions we'll be addressing as we work together. Now before you know for sure whether you want to go ahead with the assessment, I bet there are some questions that you'd like to ask me."*

Client: (Short pause—looks at SF directly.) *"Just one really. Why do you do this kind of work?"*

SF: *"Hmmm . . . Well of course assessment is my job and I support myself by doing it. I find it interesting and I like to help people. But to be honest I do it mainly because it's very moving and I get a lot from every assessment."*

Client: *"How so?"*

---

[6] All excerpts and case examples presented in this document are used with permission of the clients, and identifying information is greatly altered.

SF: *"Well like with you today . . . I've never talked to some-
            one who's struggling with exactly your set of problems.
            And by the end of the assessment I hope to understand
            a lot better what it means to be you. That will help me
            as a person."*

Client: *"Oh I see. It's like you get to live a bunch of different lives."*

SF: *"Exactly, and it really feels like a privilege to be able to
            do so."*

This interchange may seem quite shocking to assessors who
are used to turning questions back on clients (e.g., "Why do
you ask?") or who have been taught to conceal information
about themselves from clients. However, this type of interchange places the client-assessor relationship in a collaborative context, again setting the stage for clients to integrate the
MMPI-2 findings presented in the feedback session.

The question above was asked by a client who functions at a
relatively high level, but many clients come up with some ver-
sion of the question, "Why do you do this?" Other frequent
questions concern my professional credentials, or how I got
started doing assessment. I have found it works best to give
brief but genuine answers, so that clients feel that I am emotionally present and that I take them seriously.

Some colleagues just beginning to utilize the collaborative
assessment model report that clients never ask questions
about them. Clients are most likely to query the assessor if the
assessor assumes that they will have questions and implicitly
communicates that it is quite natural and even healthy for
clients to wonder about the assessor. After all, why should
clients trust an unfamiliar assessor, without first asking questions about credentials, etc.?

Completing the Assessment Contract

In the last portion of the interview, the assessor first summarizes the procedures to be followed and the responsibilities of
both client and assessor. Points that should be covered are:

➤ When and where will the client take the MMPI-2?

➤ When and where will the feedback session take place?

➤ Who will be present at the feedback session?

➤ Will there be written feedback, or only oral feedback?

➤ How much and when is the client expected to pay the assessor?

Some of these points (especially fee issues) have probably been discussed with the client earlier but are reviewed at this point. Again, the client is encouraged to take an active role in negotiating the time of testing sessions, feedback sessions, etc., thereby demonstrating her/his importance to the assessment. Obviously, if the client has been referred by another professional, that person too will have a say about the timing and structure of feedback sessions. In the rare case that a client and referring professional disagree about who should be present at the feedback session or whether there should be a written report, I ask the two of them to negotiate these points and to let me know their decision.

Introducing the MMPI-2

In the last minutes of the initial interview, the assessor shows the MMPI-2 booklet and answer sheet to the client, and summarizes the test instructions. Typically I emphasize the importance of the client's responding to all the test items and working with good attention and concentration. I encourage the client to take short breaks if need be. Then, either the client proceeds to complete the MMPI-2 at that time, or returns at another time to do so.

Table 1 summarizes the steps in the initial interview of the MMPI-2 intervention.

Table 1

The Initial Interview

Build rapport with the client
- Make small talk
- Introduce the initial interview from a collaborative perspective
- Listen attentively, with genuine interest and concern

Help the client frame questions to be addressed by the assessment

Collect background information
- Begin with information relevant to the client's questions
- Ask permission to collect all other information and explain why you need it

If the client is not participating fully, inquire about the client's reservations about the assessment

Inquire about past assessment experiences and listen for past hurts
- Show genuine interest in past experiences
- Demonstrate empathy for the client's vulnerability and hurt
- Clearly state the shortcomings of the past assessment procedures
- Offer an assessment contract which addresses the past hurtful experiences
- Ask to be alerted if the client feels mistreated

Restate the assessment questions
- Invite the client to modify the questions
- Invite the client to pose further questions as they arise

Encourage the client to ask questions of the assessor

Complete the contract for the assessment

Introduce the MMPI-2 to the client

Case example — Ms. C

Ms. C was a 24-year-old woman referred by her probation officer, Ms. Gomez, for an MMPI-2 assessment. (Ms. Gomez routinely referred all new clients to me for an MMPI-2.) At the time of the assessment, Ms. C had completed one year of a five-year probation sentence. She was convicted of assault with a dangerous weapon for holding a knife to a man's throat at a party after he refused to have sex with her. Ms. C was intoxicated at the time of this incident and had a history of severe alcohol abuse dating to age 12. The terms of her pro-

---

bation were that she complete a two-week outpatient treatment for alcoholism, abstain from alcohol and drugs and have periodic urine tests to verify this, attend meetings of Alcoholics Anonymous, and stay out of trouble.

Ms. C was initially quite skeptical of me and the MMPI-2 and cynical about the likelihood of the assessment proving useful to her. This led to some tense moments early in the initial interview, as I attempted to engage Ms. C in generating questions for the assessment:

SF: *"So what things would you like to learn about yourself from the assessment?"*

Ms. C: (with obvious hostility) *"I can't believe that any test can tell me anything I don't already know about myself."*

SF: *"Yes, I know it seems strange. I probably wouldn't believe it myself if I hadn't seen it work so many times."*

Ms. C: *"Ms. Gomez said I was just afraid of what I might learn."*

SF: *"What do you think?"*

Ms. C: (less hostile) *"I think the whole idea is just pretty weird, that's all. And I was pissed that I have to go through yet another thing for this damn probation. But you say that people can actually get answers to questions they have about themselves?"*

SF: *"That's right. In my experience the test can be pretty helpful to people who are trying to change things in their lives. Are there some things that you've been wondering about yourself that you'd like to understand better?"*

Several minutes later, as Ms C seemed to become interested in the assessment, her first set of reservations came up in our discussion:

Ms. C: *"So after you get these results on a person, what happens then?"*

SF: *"Just what I told you. I'd write a brief report for you and Ms. Gomez, and you and I would get together again to talk about the results and the questions you had for the assessment."*

Ms. C: *"So your report—does it go in my file?"*

SF: *"You know, I'm really not sure. I've never asked Ms. Gomez. But if I were to guess I would say yes. Does that bother you?"*

Ms. C: *"I'm so sick of everybody knowing every little thing about me. I was in court last year for this thing that happened—that's why I'm on probation. And I had to answer all these questions that were nobody's business, but my lawyer said I had to or the judge would throw the book at me."*

SF: *"I wouldn't like that either. You must have felt really exposed. So does this assessment feel just like that felt?"*

To my surprise, my simple acknowledgment of Ms. C's vulnerability was enough to allow her to pose several questions for the MMPI-2:

1.   *If I start drinking after probation, will it cause me problems?*

2.   *Am I a danger to society?*

3.   *Am I manipulative?*

As I collected background information, Ms. C explained that these questions came from feedback she had received from counselors during her outpatient alcohol treatment. She said that at first she had dismissed these statements, but lately found she was bothered by them. She was determined not to get in legal trouble again, but hated the idea that she would have to stop drinking alcohol forever. Her friends drank heavily and she felt she would lose them if she couldn't drink after her probation. Also she had been drinking for so long that she "wouldn't know who she was" if she stopped drinking. Last, she felt misunderstood when the alcohol counselors told her she was "manipulative" and a "danger to society." She had never thought of herself that way and wanted a second opinion to see if she should take such statements seriously.

As often happens, when Ms. C sensed that I was genuinely interested in her goals, she became freer with me in the interview. Then a second set of reservations spontaneously arose, related to a past assessment experience:

SF: *"Okay, those are good questions. I'm sure that the testing will be able to say something about all of those. Any other things you've been wondering about?"*

Ms. C: *"You know, I had some testing once before."*

SF: *"Really? When was that?"*

Ms. C: *"In ninth grade. There was this guy, Mr. Clay, doing his internship, or whatever, as a school counselor. I was always in trouble so they made me go talk to him every week. Well one day he asked me. . . . he was taking some course on testing . . . and asked if he could give me some test he was learning about. I said yes. I can't remember the name. I looked at inkblots. It had a funny name."*

SF: *"That sounds like the Rorschach."*

Ms. C: *"That was it. The Rorschach."*

SF: *"So how was that experience for you?"*

Ms. C: *"Weird. We did the test . . . it took a couple of hours I think . . . and afterwards Mr. Clay looked kind of scared of me. . . . You know like he just wanted to get away. I asked him how I had done and he said he had never seen responses like mine before and would have to talk to his professor. Then shortly after that he finished his internship and I never saw him again."*

SF: *"So did you get any more feedback about the Rorschach results?"*

Ms. C: *"I don't think so. I only saw him maybe once after that and we didn't talk about it."*

SF: *"What was that like for you—that you didn't find out more about the test results?"*

Ms. C: *"Well I've always wondered what it showed . . . and I remember that look on his face . . . like he had seen a ghost or something. It's weird. . . . I still remember it to this day."*

SF: *"Well I can imagine it felt weird—to spend several hours taking a test, to see the person have some obvious reaction, and then to never talk about the results. And then on top of that to have the person disappear right after."*

As we talked further about Ms. C's previous assessment experience, I was careful not to criticize Mr. Clay, of whom she obviously had been fond. But I repeated my promise to give her feedback about the MMPI-2 results. When I returned to the topic of what she would like from the assessment, Ms. C posed another question for the assessment:

  4.   *Why do I never seem to get along with men?*

Notice that this fourth question was at a deeper level—it came from Ms. C herself and not from something someone had told her. As I collected background information, I could see that Ms. C was sincerely distressed about her numerous dissatisfying and tumultuous relationships with men and genuinely wondered why she had so much difficulty in relationships. She wavered between blaming the men she had been involved with and blaming herself for being so "stupid" to get involved with them.

Last, Ms. C and I agreed that I would consider another question, which Ms. Gomez had asked that I address:

5. *Is Ms. C a good candidate for psychotherapy, and if so what kind?*

Ms. Gomez had previously shared this question with Ms. C. Ms. C explained that she herself had no wish to seek psychotherapy, but that Ms. Gomez felt it might be a good idea and had even offered to pay for it with probation department funds.

Notice that all the assessment questions were specific enough to be addressed by the MMPI-2, but broad enough to give me room to decide how to answer them in a feedback session. Questions of this nature are ideal for an MMPI-2 intervention.

After the session, when I reflected further on my interactions with Ms. C, I sensed several deeper questions that seemed to be indicated in her overt goals for the assessment: "Am I a bad person?" "Am I hopeless?" "Am I as bad as they tell me I am?" "Is there something in me that scares other people?" "Are my views about myself totally wrong?" "Must I distrust myself?" I knew that whatever my eventual answers to the five assessment questions, Ms. C would also be listening carefully to my opinions about these underlying questions.

Step 2. Preparing for the Feedback Session

Interpreting and Organizing the Test Findings

After the client completes the MMPI-2, the test is scored and the scores plotted, and the assessor prepares an outline of the results. At this point, all results are considered, whether or not they bear on the questions the client and referring professional posed for the assessment. The rationale here is that results may be useful in determining how to talk to the client about the MMPI-2, even if the content of all results is not reported.

Table 2

Organizing the Content of an MMPI-2 Interpretation

1. **Consistency:** Did the client respond consistently to the test items?

2. **Test-Taking Attitude:** Comment on the validity of the profile and the probable mindset of the client when responding to the test. If the profile is guarded, quantify the defensiveness (mild, moderate, severe) and discuss its nature (e.g., claiming excessive virtue, downplaying problems).

3. **Distress and Disturbance:** Quantify (no, mild, moderate, or severe) the levels of emotional distress and emotional disturbance indicated by the profile. (Emotional distress = reported depression, agitation, and anxiety; psychological disturbance = pathology as judged by mental-health professionals.)

4. **Major Symptoms:** What are the major symptoms and signs the client would report or you would notice in a brief interview? These may include major factors in the client's history.

5. **Underlying Personality:** If you could observe the client over a longer period of time or talk to persons who know her/him well, what personality traits would become obvious? (You may choose to describe the client's typical behavior in relationships here, or make a separate paragraph.)

6. **Behavior in Relationships (Optional):** How does the client manage anger, dependency needs, intimacy, and sexuality in relationships?

7. **Implications for Treatment:** What type of treatment is preferred for this type of client? (Be specific if you can.) What difficulties, if any, are anticipated in the beginning, middle, or ending stages of psychotherapy?

8. **Impression:** What diagnoses (either general or specific) are suggested by the profile? You may list several, including "rule/out diagnoses" (diagnoses that are not the highest probability, but that should be considered in further evaluations of the client).

9. **Recommendations:** If the profile leads to clear recommendations, list them here.

   Do not feel compelled to make recommendations.

Graham (1993), Greene (1991), and Butcher and Williams (1992) provide outlines for organizing comprehensive MMPI-2 results. I like to use the interpretive outline in Table 2, which is a modification of one developed by Zigfrids Stelmachers, Ph.D., of Hennepin County Medical Center, Minneapolis, MN.

Case example — Ms. C

Let us apply this outline to Ms. C's MMPI-2 results (see Figure 2).

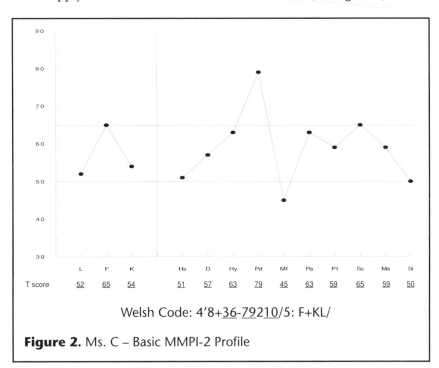

	L	F	K	Hs	D	Hy	Pd	Mf	Pa	Pt	Sc	Ma	Si
T score	52	65	54	51	57	63	79	45	63	59	65	59	50

Welsh Code: 4'8+36-79210/5: F+KL/

Figure 2. Ms. C – Basic MMPI-2 Profile

Table 3 provides a summary of Ms. C's MMPI-2 results, organized according to Stelmachers's outline. Code-type information is from Butcher and Williams (1992), Greene (1991), Graham (1993), and Webb and McNamara (1978). Auxiliary scores are listed when they were used in the interpretation.

Notice that this is a "blind" interpretation of the MMPI-2 protocol that has not been modified on the basis of my interactions with Ms. C. For example, if considering only the MMPI-2 profile, one would be quite pessimistic about Ms. C's capacity

---

Table 3

Ms. C - MMPI-2 Results

1. **Consistency:**
   - Items answered carefully and consistently (VRIN = 7, TRIN = 9)

2. **Test-Taking Attitude:**
   - Valid profile (L, F, K ok)
   - Neither a defended nor a particularly unguarded profile, but admitted to some problems (L, K, F)

3. **Distress and Disturbance:**
   - Mild emotional distress (Scale F = 65T, Scale 7 = 59T, ANX = 56T, DEP = 54T, A = 54T)
   - Moderate character disturbance (4-8, 4-3, 4-6 code types, moderate elevation)

4. **Major Symptoms:**
   - Very angry (Scale 4, 4-6 code type)
     but difficulties expressing anger directly (Scale 3, Scale 5)
     likely to hold anger in and then explode (4-3, 4-6 code types)
     likely to express anger indirectly (4-low 5)
     anger at authority figures (Pd2=77T)
   - Antisocial behavior (4-8 code type)
     troubles with the law
     erratic, unpredictable behavior
     poor judgment, promiscuity
     alcohol and drug abuse highly likely
     antisocial acts may have an unusual quality (Scale 8)
   - Underachievement (4-8 code type)
   - Inability to sustain close relationships (4-8, 4-low 5-6)
   - Likely to come from family with lots of conflict (4-8, 4-3, 4-6)
   - Suicidal thoughts and attempts (4-8, 4-3)

5. **Underlying Personality:**
   - Deep feelings of insecurity (4-8 code type)
   - Immature and self-indulgent (4, 4-3, 4-6)
   - Exaggerated needs for attention and affection (4-3, 4-8)
   - Suspicious of motives of others (4-6)
   - Sensitive (6)

---

for any insight into herself. By contrast, during my interview with her, I distinctly felt that she was wondering about the trouble she was in. Further, her fourth assessment question ("Why do I have so much conflict in my relationships with

Table 3, *continued*

6. **Behavior in Relationships:**
   - Manipulative (Scale 4)
     won't ask directly for needs to be met (4-3, 4-low 5-6)
   - Demanding, sullen, argumentative (4-3, 4-8)
   - Critical, vindictive (4-6, 4-3)
   - Sensitive to rejection (4-8, 4-6)
   - Strikes out as a defense against being hurt (4-8, 4-6)
   - Externalizes blame for relationship problems (Scale 4, Scale 6)
   - Hostile when criticized (4-3, 4-6)
   - Chooses partners who are inadequate in order to feel
     in control (4-8)

7. **Implications for Treatment:**
   - Many difficulties anticipated with insight-oriented therapy
     not in enough distress to want treatment
     similar code types typically uninterested in therapy
     will have difficulties trusting therapist
     may use sessions to complain about others rather than
       examine self
     may easily feel hurt/rejected by therapist
     similar clients are passive-aggressive with therapists
   - Might benefit from group therapy without too much
     confrontation

8. **Impression:**
   - Mixed personality disorder with antisocial, narcissistic,
     passive-aggressive features
   - R/O psychosis (4-8, 4-6)

9. **Recommendations:**
   - Monitor alcohol and drug use
   - Monitor acting-out behaviors
   - Monitor suicidal thoughts
   - Wait until she is more distressed before suggesting therapy?
   - Refer for group therapy and contract for a minimum
     number of sessions?

men?") seems to reflect her ability to be observant about herself. When I am compiling the test results, I try hard to keep myself from being influenced by the interview, so that the client and I may puzzle together over "pure" test results in the collaborative atmosphere of the feedback session.

Tailoring the MMPI-2 Feedback to the Client

Once I understand the MMPI-2 results and have organized them in an outline, I consider the best way of talking to the particular client about the results. In this step I am guided by five major queries:

> ➤ How do the MMPI-2 findings relate to the client's goals?

> ➤ What are the most important findings of the MMPI-2?

> ➤ To what extent is the client likely to already know about and agree with the MMPI-2 findings?

> ➤ How much new information is the client likely to be able to integrate in the feedback session?

> ➤ What is likely to happen if the client becomes overwhelmed or is presented with findings that are greatly discrepant from her/his current self-concept?

Let us first consider each of these queries in general:

1. How do the MMPI-2 findings relate to the client's goals? The client's questions and goals provide an essential way of organizing information for the feedback session; they also indicate what the client wants and is ready to know from the MMPI-2. I consider each of the client's questions and try to answer it for myself, using only the MMPI-2 results. Typically there are many other answers/hypotheses that could be offered based on my observations of the client or knowledge of background information. At this stage I am careful to use only information derived from the testing. If the MMPI-2 provides several possible answers to a client's question, I note all of them. If I find no relationship between the MMPI-2 results and a particular question, I note that also.

2. What are the most important findings? This query helps me prioritize the wealth of information that can be derived from any MMPI-2 profile. Typically it is impossible (and inadvisable) to tell clients everything that can be inferred or hypothesized from the MMPI-2 regarding their questions; in most cases this would overwhelm them. Thus, I force myself to go back and consider the various answers and hypotheses I generated in response to the client's questions. Using all the information available to me at the time (from history, conversations with the referring professional, etc.), I force myself to choose five statements that I feel will have the most beneficial impact on the client, at the time of the assessment. Often, I am helped at this stage by any sense I have of the broader goals underlying the client's assessment questions.

3. Will the client already know about or agree with the MMPI-2 findings? First I make a judgment of the client's general level of psychological awareness, as indicated by the MMPI-2 code types and scale scores. Next, I go back to the findings I have listed in response to queries 1 and 2 and classify each into one of three types of information:

•**Level 1 Information:** Findings that verify clients' usual ways of thinking about themselves and that will be easily accepted in the feedback session. When told this information, a client will generally say, "I already know that."

•**Level 2 Information:** Findings that modify or amplify clients' usual ways of thinking about themselves, but that are unlikely to be seen as threats to self-esteem or self-perceptions. When told this type of information, a client might say, "I've never thought about myself quite this way before, but I can see how what you're saying fits."

•**Level 3 Information:** Findings that are so novel or discrepant from clients' usual ways of thinking about themselves that they are likely to be rejected in feedback sessions. Typically, such information would be expected to threaten a client, mobilizing characteristic defense mechanisms.

4. How open is the client to new information? Some clients are in so fragile an emotional state when they come for an assessment that they are unable to integrate a great deal of new information. Such clients may generate a number of questions to be answered by the MMPI-2 but are unable to tolerate complex answers to numerous questions.

5. How will the client react to discrepant or highly novel information? It is always good to anticipate how a client is likely to react if overwhelmed during the feedback session. This step involves hypothesizing about the client's usual coping strategies and defense mechanisms. Is the client likely to intellectualize, deny, become hostile and projecting, or dissociate in the face of anxiety?

Using Test Results to Facilitate Empathy

At this point you may be wondering how an assessor can possibly judge what is most important to tell clients, what findings clients are likely to accept, how much clients can integrate, and how clients will react when faced with information that threatens their usual identities and self-esteem. To answer these questions the assessor must rely on empathy—the process of "sensing oneself into" a client's experience to accurately apprehend the client's thoughts and feelings.[7]

An assessor uses many types of information to achieve an empathic understanding of a client in a session: the client's posture or facial expression, tone of voice, or subjective description of inner experience. However, empathy is possible even if a client is not actually present; skilled assessors may use historical information, previous impressions of a client, test findings, and even the client's initial assessment questions to "put themselves in a client's shoes." Once this empathic stance has been achieved, the process of planning an MMPI-2 feedback session is relatively straightforward; the assessor must simply ask herself or himself: "If I were this client, what would be the best way to talk to me about these MMPI-2 results?"

---

[7] Notice that this use of the word empathy is different from our lay use of the word, which more resembles "sympathy" or "compassion." Thus, it may not feel compassionate to judge that a client wishes to shirk all responsibility and be taken care of by others, but it may be quite empathic.

Having a deep understanding of a client's MMPI-2 test results can greatly facilitate empathy. The MMPI-2 has a wealth of information about the client's personality style, ego strength, defenses, and awareness of psychological issues. And as assessors gain experience giving MMPI-2 feedback to clients with different types of test scores, they will better predict clients' responses in a feedback session. Table 4 presents some observations about elevations on the MMPI-2 basic scales and their implications for test feedback sessions. These are offered to aid assessors' empathy. Table 4 provides answers to queries 3-5 above, for each of the MMPI-2 basic scales.

Tables 4 and 5 provide some basic examples of how to anticipate clients' reactions to test feedback; however, with complex MMPI-2 code types the assessor needs to understand the gestalt of the entire profile to make such predictions. Thus the assessor will need to refer to the outline of MMPI-2 results (Table 2) in deciding not only *what* to say to the client, but *how* to say it. And all information from the MMPI-2—not just the basic scales—can be useful in tailoring a feedback session to a particular client. For example, the MMPI-2 Content Scales (Butcher, Graham, Williams, & Ben-Porath, 1990) are particularly useful in judging whether clients are aware of different findings from the MMPI-2. The items on the Content Scales are extremely face valid, so if a client achieves an elevation on a particular scale, one may be confident that the client has knowingly admitted to the problems represented on that scale and will easily accept an interpretation of that scale.

Of course, if testing besides the MMPI-2 is available, this too can help in planning the feedback session. For example, the assessor should plan to speak differently to a client with an IQ of 135 than to a client with an IQ of 85. And if a client has a Performance IQ of 110 and a Verbal IQ of 85, the assessor might plan to present the MMPI-2 graph to the client as a visual cue while giving the results in simple verbal statements. Again, all information available on the client can be used to "put oneself in the client's shoes" and then tailor the feedback session to the client.

Table 4

Some Implications of MMPI-2 Scale Elevations for Test Feedback

Cannot Say (?)
A high number of omissions suggests evasiveness, lack of cooperation with the testing, or "pickiness." In the last case, the client may react to anxiety by focusing on small details in the test feedback and either challenging them or asking the assessor to elaborate. Beware of getting sidetracked in the feedback session.

L
Elevations suggest an unwillingness or inability to self-disclose. Such clients have little psychological awareness and rigid character defenses, and are easily threatened by information that challenges their view of themselves as "nice" people. When emotionally stressed, they tend to react with denial and sometimes hostility. (Look elsewhere in the profile for signs of anger.)

F
Elevations may indicate fragility and weak ego strength. Such clients are easily overwhelmed and can incorporate a limited amount of new information. They may have intense emotional reactions to test feedback. It can be useful to have family members or friends close by to help support the client after the feedback session.

K
As with elevations on ? and L, elevations on K suggest that the client has reservations about participating in the assessment and is concerned about disclosing information that might be socially undesirable. Alternatively, the client may have limited psychological awareness and may minimize problems, even to her- or himself. When confronted with test feedback that challenges their self-concepts, these clients typically reject or deny the importance of such feedback.

Scale 1
Clients with elevations on Scale 1 often lack psychological insight and prefer medical or physical explanations for problems. They become quite defensive when medical problems are attributed to psychological causes, reacting with denial and hostility. The assessor may gain credence by emphasizing the use of the MMPI-2 in medical settings, and by discussing how stress influences "real" medical conditions.

Scale 2
Clients with moderate or high elevations on Scale 2 readily admit to problems; however, they are often unaware of many interpersonal issues that show up elsewhere in the MMPI-2 protocol (e.g., anger). Such clients may focus exclusively on "negative" feedback and become

Table 4, *continued*

despairing and pessimistic when overwhelmed. At the end of the feedback session, it is often good to ask these clients to summarize what was said, so the assessor may correct any negative distortions. Clients with mild elevations on Scale 2 are sometimes unaware of being depressed and are quite surprised when such an interpretation is made. (Look at scores on DEP, and D1 to judge client awareness of depression.)

Scale 3
Clients with elevations on Scale 3 lack psychological awareness, especially of anger and anxiety, and are resistant to psychological interpretations of problems. When overwhelmed by test feedback, they react with denial or confusion. Such clients respond well to concrete suggestions and recommendations.

Scale 4
Clients with elevations on Scale 4 externalize responsibility and have little insight into their own contributions to their problems. A direct, "no-nonsense" approach is often best for giving feedback to such clients. When confronted they may try to turn the discussion to complaints about others or may react with angry denials.

Scale 6
Elevations suggest extreme sensitivity and these clients usually have a great interest in receiving test feedback. Although they are quite perceptive about other people, clients with Scale 6 elevations often have little insight into their own contribution to interpersonal problems. They are easily threatened by feedback that is inconsistent with their self-concepts and react with criticism, hostility, and flat rejections of test findings. It is important to use neutral, nonjudgmental terms when giving feedback to these clients and to be on the lookout for negative distortions of what one says.

Scale 7
Elevations may indicate a readiness to admit to problems, but such clients usually can incorporate very little test feedback. They typically defend by intellectualizing and may obsess about minor details of the feedback. The assessor should present a calm, steady demeanor and explain test results in a concrete, down-to-earth manner. Tie results to real-life examples as much as possible and be wary of being drawn into intellectual discussions.

Scale 8
Clients with elevations on Scale 8 are often easily confused in feedback sessions and grow withdrawn, tangential, and inattentive when presented with too much information. They have a tendency to distort what is said by the assessor, and it is good to ask them to repeat findings at the end of the feedback session.

Scale 9
Clients with elevations on Scale 9 are easily overwhelmed by test feedback. They have short attention spans and are likely to go off on tangents. They externalize responsibility and may become hostile if their defenses are

Table 4, *continued*

severely challenged in feedback sessions. Clients with low scores on Scale 9 have little energy and become hopeless if too much information is presented in the feedback session. Recommendations for such clients must be kept few and simple; they become lethargic and despairing if asked to do too many new things.

Scale 0
Clients with elevations on Scale 0 tend to decline feedback sessions, but may agree to them if encouraged. Like clients with elevations on Scale 2, these clients readily admit to problems and resist discussion of possible strengths in their personalities. When stressed, they often react with skepticism and withdrawal. It is good to check at the end of the feedback session for negative distortions of test findings.

Table 5

Using MMPI-2 Basic Scales to Anticipate Typical Client Reactions to Feedback Sessions

Scale	Level of Psychological Awareness	Easily Overwhelmed?	Typical Reactions When Overwhelmed
High ?	——	——	avoidance, "pickiness"
High L	poor	——	denial, hostility
High F	——	yes	intense emotional reactions
High K	poor	——	minimization, denial
High 1	poor	——	denial, hostility, somatization
High 2	good	yes	despair, pessimism
High 3	poor	——	denial, confusion
High 4	poor	——	blaming, anger
High 6	poor	——	blaming, anger, disbelief
High 7	good	yes	intellectualization
High 8	——	yes	confusion, withdrawal
High 9	poor	yes	distractibility, hostility
Low 9	——	yes	lethargy, despair
High 0	good	——	withdrawal, skepticism

Getting Emotional Support before the Feedback Session

A final, but very important part of an assessor's preparation for a feedback session involves pausing to notice anxiety about the upcoming session and seeking support from peers or a supervisor. Such support is often a crucial factor in whether the feedback session goes smoothly.

There are many good reasons why assessors become anxious before a feedback session. They may accurately sense the great impact such sessions have on a client and feel their responsibility to make the feedback session a positive experience for the client. Anxiety is likely if the assessor feels insecure about her/his ability to deal with unanticipated events in the session. Assessor anxiety seems to increase (appropriately) when the MMPI-2 suggests that a client may become belligerent or violent when challenged. Finally, assessors may worry about damaging the positive relationship they already have with a client and referring professional. These issues are worthy of discussion before the assessor undertakes a feedback session.

When I need support before a feedback session, I often roleplay the situation I most fear with a colleague (e.g., a client's rejecting every test finding I present). In this way I explore how I would handle such a situation. Sometimes in talking things through I realize that I need tangible support during or right after a session, e.g., someone nearby to assist me should a client become violent or extremely distressed. I then arrange for this. Last, I remind myself that collaborative assessment generally precludes disastrous feedback sessions, by treating clients respectfully and involving them in the assessment.

Case example — Ms. C

We now return to the example of Ms. C (Figure 2, Table 3) to consider how to give her feedback about her MMPI-2 results. Table 6 summarizes my notes answering the five preparatory queries.

Table 6

Preparatory Notes for Ms. C's MMPI-2 Feedback Session

Answers to Assessment Goals and Questions
1. *If I start drinking after probation, will it cause me problems?*
   Yes, high risk of continued alcohol abuse leading to problems with law, poor judgment, etc.

2. *Am I a danger to society?*
   Possibility of doing things that are dangerous to others or self, especially as an expression of intense anger.

3. *Am I manipulative?*
   Probably tries to get dependency needs met indirectly, without asking. Angry and entitled when others don't anticipate needs. Likely to express anger indirectly. Probably reads people well.

4. *Why do I never seem to get along with men?*
   • Passive-aggressive: probably comes off as critical and vindictive.
   • Sensitive to rejection: easily gets feelings hurt and lashes out.
   • Probably chooses partners who are inadequate and then gets angry.
   • Suspicious: difficult time trusting, likes to be in control.

5. *Is Ms. C a good candidate for psychotherapy, and if so what kind?*
   Many difficulties anticipated. Group therapy could help provide her with a non-alcoholic support group, but it will be difficult to get her to attend due to her cynicism and distrust.

Most Important Findings (in order of importance)
1. Anger: high amount and problems expressing directly

2. High risk of acting out

3. Relationship problems: wants to be taken care of but reluctant to ask directly for nurturance, support

4. Underlying insecurity and low self-esteem

5. Sensitive to rejection: lashes out ("I'll reject you before you reject me.")

Client Psychological Awareness
General: Probably tuned in to others, but not very aware of self.

Level 1 information:
   • anger and disappointment in relationships
   • anger at authority figures
   • tendency to act out, not think through consequences of actions
   • distrust, sensitivity to others' feelings
   • not open to psychotherapy

Table 6, *continued*

Level 2 information:
- amount of anger inside
- problems expressing anger directly
- lashing out as a protection against getting hurt
- difficulty asking directly for needs to be met
- tendency to get involved with inadequate partners

Level 3 information:
- underlying dependency
- underlying insecurity and low self-esteem
- sensitivity to rejection
- tendency to select inadequate partners so as to feel in control

Openness to New Information
- Could get overwhelmed if character defenses are breached.
- Will reject information if she feels condemned or judged by authority.

Reactions If Overwhelmed by Highly Discrepant Information
Probably would lash out or indirectly retaliate. Could simply deny or discount test feedback.

To discuss the case in point, I felt some mild anxiety before the feedback session with Ms. C, in part because I would be confirming some statements she had found injurious during her treatment for alcoholism. I was fairly confident that I could answer her first three questions in a way that would be beneficial to her, but I was aware that these questions were loaded with affect. I also was anxious about the possibility of Ms. C's growing hostile if she felt threatened by the test results. I disclosed my feelings to a colleague who also works collaboratively with clients. We discussed how I would handle the session if Ms. C grew hostile, and I role-played answering the first three questions. Last, we discussed my own behavior when I am anxious: I tend to become a bit distant and act like an all-knowing "expert" rather than a collaborator. Forewarned about my own tendency to do this—which would exacerbate any anxiety on Ms. C's part—I felt much more confident about the upcoming feedback session.

Step 3. The Feedback Session

The final and perhaps most important part of the MMPI-2 intervention is the feedback session, which lasts approximately 60 minutes for an individual client. Occasionally, you will find that more time is needed. There are many similarities between the feedback procedures described below and those used by Erdberg (1979), Butcher (1990), and Lewak, Marks, and Nelson (1990).

Goals

The overriding goal of feedback sessions is to have a therapeutic interaction with clients. To achieve this goal, the assessor strives to:

➤ Ease clients' initial anxiety about the feedback session

➤ Re-establish the collaborative tone of the assessment

➤ Educate clients further about the MMPI-2

➤ Answer the agreed-upon questions for the assessment

➤ Tie test findings to real-life examples

➤ Engage clients in corroborating or modifying test findings

➤ Avoid overwhelming clients or triggering major defensive reactions

➤ Support clients' feelings resulting from new awareness

➤ Correct any distortions clients may have about test findings

➤ Provide a means for clients to deal with questions and reactions that arise after the feedback session

The Interpersonal Quality of the Session

The interpersonal quality of the feedback session may be the most crucial element in whether the session goes well. As discussed earlier, the therapeutic model of assessment promotes an interpersonal "tone" that is both collaborative and supportive. In the feedback session the underlying communication from the assessor to the client should be something like this: "I, the assessor, am an expert on the MMPI-2 and you, the client, are an expert on yourself. I fully expect that you already know (on some level) much of what I will be telling you today. My job is mainly to reorganize or retell your inner experience in new language, to help you find new solutions to old problems. I fully expect to learn new things about the MMPI-2, about you, and about myself from our dialogue. Thank you for the privilege of sharing your inner experience for this short while." I do not speak these words directly to clients. However, I try to demonstrate this attitude in everything I do in the session—my tone of voice and body language, the words I choose to present findings, and my response when a client modifies or rejects a finding. Many of the procedures elaborated below are the operational expressions of this collaborative/supportive tone. It is more important to keep this overall tone in mind than to rigidly follow the steps outlined below. Likewise, you could perform all the procedures here while maintaining a non-collaborative, unsupportive stance with a client. I would expect that such a feedback session would have no therapeutic benefit for the client.

Setting the Client at Ease

Most clients are fairly anxious when they come for an MMPI-2 feedback session, although not all are consciously aware of it. Addressing their anxiety at the beginning of the session typically helps clients to pay attention, listen non-defensively, and fully participate as collaborators in the feedback session. I usually begin by showing interest in what a client has been experiencing while anticipating the MMPI-2 findings. I then listen carefully, aware of the sensitivity of the client's position, and demonstrate my empathic understanding to the client:

Assessor: *"So what's it like coming in today for the test results?"*

Client: *"I'm excited about it. I'm really looking forward to hear-ing what the test has to say. But I tossed and turned a lot last night in bed."*

Assessor: *"So it's exciting, but perhaps a little nerve-wracking too. . ."*

                              or

Assessor: *"How are you feeling today?"*

Client: *"I'm pretty terrified that you're going to tell me some-thing I don't want to know."*

Assessor: *"Is there anything in particular you're afraid I might say?"*

Client: *"Not really, it's just difficult not knowing what's coming."*

Assessor: *"Yes, isn't that hard? A lot of people feel scared about that. And then I'm remembering—you had that really bad experience when you got MMPI results from Dr._____ two years ago."*

Client: *"Yes, I guess that's part of it. Even though this feels that it's totally different, I find myself dreading what you'll say to me."*

As the second excerpt illustrates, a client's anxiety at the beginning of the feedback session may result from some reser-vation the client has about the assessment. Even if the same reservation has been talked about during the initial interview, it may deserve further discussion, following the principles that were presented earlier (pp. 17-20).

Another way of breaking the ice in the feedback session is to inquire about the client's experience in taking the MMPI-2 (if the two of you have not spoken since the test was administered.) Once again, it is important to listen carefully and appreciate the client's point of view:

Assessor: *"So what was it like taking the MMPI-2?"*

Client: *"Well, it dragged on and on. I was sick of it by the end!"*

Assessor: *"Yes, it certainly has a lot of items."*

Client: *"Do you really need them all to answer those questions we asked?"*

Assessor: *"Yes, I'm afraid so. But I'm hoping that after our session today, you'll feel it was worth the time you spent taking the test."*

Re-establishing the Collaborative Relationship

Typically a client's anxiety will decrease even further if you then review the purpose and format of the feedback session in a way that re-establishes the collaborative tone of the assessment. By reminding the client of her/his role as an active participant, you decrease the client's feelings of powerlessness concerning the feedback session. There are several steps to doing this:

1. Remind the client that the purpose of the feedback session is to answer the assessment questions. I usually state this directly and then read the list of assessment questions to the client and ask if she/he would like to add any other questions at that time. Sometimes, clients put a previously unstated concern into words, perhaps because of the increased anxiety they feel while awaiting the test results.

2. Frame the MMPI-2 as a communication from the client to you and the referring professional. Explain that the MMPI-2 is just another way for people to tell things about themselves. If the profile is unguarded, this may be a good time to thank the client for "telling so much" about herself or himself. If the profile is highly guarded, this is the opportunity to talk about the client's reluctance to disclose information.

3. Explain that the client will be asked to verify findings. Tell the client that you will be "telling back what you heard" from the MMPI-2, but will be checking with the client from time to time to see if you "heard things right." This explanation signals that you will not attempt to impose some test interpretation on the client and that the client will be asked to actively participate in the feedback session.

Orienting the Client to the MMPI-2 Profile

At this point in the feedback session, it is generally good to give the client a 5-10 minute orientation to the MMPI-2; this often involves showing the basic profile sheet and explaining how to read the graph. The MMPI-2 orientation should be "tailored" to the individual client, depending on your empathic understanding of the client. For example:

➤   If the client is likely to become confused by such an orientation because of psychosis or low intelligence, eliminate the orientation entirely and proceed with test findings.

➤   If the client can handle very little new information, skip directly to answering the client's assessment questions.

➤   If the client is highly anxious, spend more time on this orientation, to give the client a chance to calm down.

➤   If the client tends to frame psychological difficulties in terms of physical complaints, emphasize that the MMPI was originally developed in a medical setting and that it has been used to study numerous medical conditions.

➤   If the client has an adequate Verbal IQ but a deficient Performance IQ, don't show the MMPI-2 profile graph; instead give the client an extensive verbal introduction to the test.

➤   If the client is skeptical of the assessment results, emphasize the strong research base underlying MMPI-2

scale interpretation and explain in detail how the
basic scales were empirically constructed.

Setting these special considerations aside for the moment,
here is the generic wording for an orientation to the MMPI-2. I
work from these words in constructing an orientation tailored
to a particular client:

> *"This is the graph of your MMPI-2 results. Let me
> teach you how to look at it. As you probably guessed, I
> don't go through and read each answer you gave to
> the items on the test. The items are grouped together
> into different scales. Each scale reflects a different type
> of problem that people can experience. Imagine lines
> running up and down the page above these numbers.*
> (Point to scale indicators.) *Each of those lines would
> be a different problem scale, and the dots here that
> I've connected by a line show your score on each of the
> ten problem scales of the MMPI.*

> *"One thing I want to say right off is that the MMPI-2
> is a problem-oriented test. It doesn't give a lot of infor-
> mation about your strengths, so let's keep that in mind
> as we go over these results.*

> *"Now each of the MMPI-2 scales was designed so that
> people not reporting a particular problem will score
> right around the 50 line here. In general, as scores get
> further away from the 50 line, the more a person is
> saying that he or she has a particular problem. And
> scores that get close to or above this 65 line are a sign
> that a person is reporting a problem that is more seri-
> ous and that may require special attention. Any ques-
> tions?*

> *"Now these scales on the left are not problem scales.
> They are scales that look at people's approach to tak-
> ing the test—whether they were trying to make them-
> selves look good or look bad on the test, and whether
> they answered the test items carefully or perhaps were*

careless or even answered randomly. Your scores on these scales show that . . . "

At this point I usually summarize briefly the results of the validity scales. In most cases, when the client has been referred voluntarily and has been enlisted as a collaborator in the assessment, the MMPI-2 profile is quite unguarded. Therefore, I explain that the client apparently did not try to look good or look bad on the MMPI-2 and that other scale scores are not distorted. Guidelines for talking to clients about invalid profiles are presented later, under the heading Special Considerations.

Answering the Client's Assessment Questions

Having oriented the client to the MMPI-2, I then begin the major task of the feedback session: answering the client's assessment questions by presenting test findings and hypotheses to the client. Often it is easy to alternate back and forth between questions and MMPI-2 scales to frame answers, especially if the questions are simple ones: *"Your first question was about how depressed you are. Well this scale here is a depression scale . . ."* or *"You were wondering why you're having so many back problems lately. Your score on this scale suggests that your back problems probably get worse when you are angry and are not aware of it . . ."* Other assessment questions are more complex and require that the assessor discuss several scale scores or code-type patterns to answer them. The order in which I present the questions and the language I use in discussing the MMPI-2 scales and code-types are highly dependent on my empathic understanding of the client. Here are some general principles:

1. Begin with something positive. In most cases clients will be more receptive to later results if you focus on a positive finding early in the feedback session.[8] It is important that such a finding be accurate; do not simply invent something to

---

[8] The major exception to this guideline is when the client's self-concept is exclusively negative. In such cases, the client will experience the positive statement as Level 3 information—i.e., an empathic break.

flatter a client. Often I simply express my authentic apprecia-
tion for the trust the client has shown by producing an
unguarded profile. Or, I may discuss a positive aspect of some
scale elevation, e.g., the sensitivity shown in a Scale 6 elevation, or the high energy level suggested by a moderate elevation on Scale 9. It is best if the positive finding can be tied to
one of the client's questions, but if it cannot, you may simply
introduce the finding as is.

2. Move from level 1 to level 2 to level 3 information.
Although the client posed assessment questions in a certain
order in the initial interview, you should reorder them in the
feedback session, according to the client's awareness of the
answer. By beginning with information the client finds famil-
iar (level 1 information), you gain credibility and the client
begins to trust the MMPI-2 as a test. Also, as clients' views of
themselves are confirmed, their anxiety decreases. They feel
relief that you will not be asking them to completely change
their existing self-representations. Most of the feedback session should be spent presenting level 2 findings to the client—
those that are not a complete surprise, but that reframe a
client's current self-concept or put new words to some previously unnamed experience.

Typically, you should present level 3 information— findings
that are highly discrepant from the client's self-concept—only
after the client has accepted and elaborated a number of level
1 and level 2 findings. Level 3 information is typically highly
anxiety-provoking for the client, and too much discussion of
level 3 findings may leave the client with negative feelings
about the feedback session. Level 3 findings are more likely to
be accepted if they are clearly tied to the client's goals for the
assessment. Another useful strategy is to distance yourself
slightly from the finding by reading it from an MMPI-2 code
book or by indicating your own surprise at the test result. In
this way the client can reject the finding without fear of creating a breach in her/his relationship with you.

3. Don't tell everything. It is essential that you carefully
select what information will be presented by considering the
feedback session preparatory queries 1 and 2 (client goals and

most important issues). Reporting too many findings typically overburdens clients. Furthermore, if you casually give findings that are not related to the client's goals for the assessment, the client is likely to feel violated and that the assessment contract has been betrayed, i.e., you have expanded the observation deck beyond the agreed-upon blueprints. One may choose to discuss a certain MMPI-2 scale, even if the client has not previously expressed curiosity about related issues. However, such decisions must be weighed carefully and every effort should be made to connect the finding to one of the client's assessment questions, if only indirectly. I stress this guideline while recognizing that it is very difficult not to tell the client everything that you know (see p. 61).

4. Tailor your language to the particular client. Never use words like "hysteria" or "psychopathic deviate" in describing the MMPI-2 scales. Instead, choose scale descriptors that will be useful in answering the client's assessment questions. For example, if a client has asked about anger management, it may be useful to describe Scale 4 as an "anger scale." Likewise, Scale 7 can be talked about as an "anxiety scale" or as a "worry scale," depending on the emphasis the assessor wishes to use in presenting results. Use simple common words whenever possible and avoid psychological jargon. Use language that is appropriate to the client's age, education, and level of intelligence. Select metaphors from the client's occupation or that otherwise fit with the client's life experience. Erdberg (1979) and Lewak, Marks, and Nelson (1990) provide good examples of MMPI scale descriptors that are easily understood by clients.

Enlisting the Client in Elaborating Test Findings

The assessor-client interactions about test findings may be the most important determinant of how the client will be affected by the feedback session. An assessor who merely reads a number of test findings to a passive client is likely to have little impact on the client; likewise, the assessor will gain little information from the client about the accuracy and generalizability of the assessor's MMPI-2 interpretations. Finally, such a distant interpersonal stance greatly protects both the assessor's and the client's feelings, making it difficult for them to have a meaningful interaction. It is much better for the assessor to cultivate an ongoing dialogue with the client about each major test finding, as follows:

1. Ask the client to verify the accuracy of the finding. You have already prepared the client for this process when introducing the feedback session (see pp. 47-48). Now after presenting a finding you may simply ask, "Does what I just said seem right to you?" Or, observe the client's reaction as you talk and use that in your inquiry, e.g., "I see that you're nodding your head. So does what I'm saying seem right?" or "Your frown seems to tell me that this result doesn't fit for you."

2. If the client confirms a result, ask for an example. This step helps the client tie abstract test findings to real life situations and therefore assists the client in integrating test findings with daily experience. Asking for an example also ensures that the client is not just agreeing with every test finding to please you or to avoid thinking deeply about what you have said. Finally, by asking for an example you can check on the client's understanding of the test result and correct this understanding if need be.

3. Ask or allow the client to modify your interpretations to make them more accurate. This step shows that you accept the client as an expert on herself or himself and are open to learning from the client. It also gives the client a feeling of being a valued participant whom you respect as a person. Last, when clients are allowed to "put their mark" on findings in the feedback session, they are more invested in and feel more ownership of the test results, and feel proud of having helped the assessor understand how the MMPI-2 scores apply specifically to them.

The following excerpt illustrates the dialogue that occurred while I was presenting level 2 information to a man with a 2-7 MMPI-2 profile:

SF: *"We also know that people with scores like yours tend to be perfectionists. They set very high standards for themselves and then are quite hard on themselves if they don't live up to those standards. (Pause.) Does that seem to fit for you?"*

Client: *"Hmmm . . . I don't know. I guess I am that way about some things, but not about others."*

SF: *"That's interesting. Can you give me an example?"*

Client: *"Well, at home I'm an incredible perfectionist. I like my house to look really good and be neat and clean and I'm never quite happy with the way it looks. But . . . well at work . . . I know I'm not doing a very good job on this latest project I told you about. And frankly I could care less."*

SF: *"And are you hard on yourself about that?"*

Client: *"Not really."*

SF: *"Well, that is interesting. So you tend to be a perfectionist about your house, but not about this one work project. What do you think makes the difference for you?"*

As this excerpt illustrates, the client-assessor dialogue about test findings helps hone more generalized test interpretations into precise, sophisticated understandings of the client. Notice how I summarized the client's modification toward the end of this excerpt, signaling that I accepted the client's input and was trying to incorporate it into my own understanding of the test results.

When the Client Rejects a Finding

Sometimes, when the above procedures are followed carefully, an entire feedback session may go by without a client ever flatly rejecting a test finding you offer. Often, however, a client will strongly disagree with a finding and assert that there is nothing to be learned from that particular finding. You may have anticipated the client's reaction because the finding was classified beforehand as level 3 information. But clients sometimes also reject test findings that we think will be accepted fairly easily. When such disagreements occur, the first thing to remember is, **the test interpretation may be wrong**. With this firmly in mind, you will avoid the greatest mistake that can be made in a feedback session—arguing with a client about a test finding. It damages the entire assessment process to try to convince a client of a certain test interpretation, even if you feel quite sure that some aspect of the interpretation is "correct." There are other options if you do not wish to drop the rejected result:

1. Repeat the test finding in different language, proposing an example of how it might show up in the client's life. It may be that the you have not explained the test interpretation clearly or have not used language that resonates with the client. Another attempt may result in the client's agreeing with the finding.

2. Ask the client if any part of the interpretation might be correct. In effect, this involves reasserting your general confidence in the MMPI-2, while inviting the client to make a major modification of the test finding. Clients may reject a finding when they feel pressed to either accept or reject it entirely.

3. Ask the client to postpone rejecting the finding and to gather additional information about it. This might involve the client speaking with friends, family, or the referring professional, or simply introspecting more about the proposed test interpretation. You can ask that the client then report back to you about the accuracy of the proposed interpretation.

4. Suggest that the client "agree to disagree" with the MMPI-2 for now, but not dismiss the test finding entirely. This is especially effective when a client is in therapy or about to enter therapy. An effective therapist can wait for a later moment, when the client may accept the disputed finding, and raise it again without giving the message of "I told you so."

A number of factors should be considered in judging whether to simply back down from a rejected test finding or whether to use one of the above strategies in hopes of the client's partially accepting the result:

➤ If you are no longer confident that the disputed result contains some truth, it is best to abandon it.

➤ If the test finding is essential to answering the client's questions for the assessment or represents a point you feel is extremely important, you may continue to discuss the result with the client.

➤ If no previous rejections have occurred and the client has accepted many other findings, you may stick with the finding longer.

➤ If the client looks panicky or confused, it may be best to state that the finding appears to be in error, ask if the client wishes to continue, and be prepared to move on to another point or begin closing the feedback session.

➤ If the client has another supportive person present in the session (e.g., a spouse, the referring professional) you can stick with a rejected finding longer, without worrying that the client will be unable to function after the feedback session.

➤ If the client has already rejected a large number of test findings, probably it is best to stop presenting findings and talk with the client about her/his feelings about the feedback session.

The following excerpt is from my feedback session with the client discussed on p. 54, the man with the 2-7 MMPI-2 profile. This interchange occurred about 40 minutes into the session and was the first time the man had completely rejected a test finding (which, incidentally, I had thought he might easily accept). He had not seemed anxious previously and I felt comfortable dialoguing with him about my interpretation.

SF: *"One other thing about people with scores like yours—they tend to approach problems by analyzing them and thinking them through intellectually. They have much more trouble identifying their feelings or using their intuition about a situation. They tend to operate more from their thoughts than from their emotions."*

Client: *"Well, the first part seems right, I am very good at analysis. But I don't agree with the second part—I always know what I feel about something. In fact my friends say I'm rather opinionated."*

SF: *"Hmmm . . . I think I haven't explained what I meant clearly. This scale isn't really about having strong opinions. It has to do with emotional awareness. Your score would suggest that you might not always know if you were sad or angry or happy or afraid—that you are stronger at knowing what you think than what you feel."*

Client: *"I still think it's wrong. I certainly know if I'm sad or angry. I'm very self-aware—more than my other friends."*

SF: *"Okay. I hear that. The MMPI-2 is certainly not always on the money. But I'm a bit puzzled. Generally this one scale is pretty accurate. Is there any part of what I said that seems to fit—about sometimes being confused about how you feel?"*

Client: *"Not at all."*

SF: *"Okay. But I wonder if you'd be willing to do one thing before we just chalk this one up as wrong."*

Client: *"What's that?"*

SF: *"Would you be willing to talk with Dr. Smith (the referring professional) about this part of the test results? He knows you much better than I do, and he might have something interesting to contribute."*

Client: *"I can do that. So you think the test might be right about this?"*

SF: *"I have no way of knowing. But it seems worth some further thought. (Long pause, observing the client's* reaction.) *Do you feel ready to go on with another test finding?"*

The Most Common Mistake: Underreporting

Having cautioned that you should never argue with a client about a rejected test finding, I will now say that most beginning assessors often make exactly the opposite mistake: They fail to tell a client about an important test finding because they incorrectly judge that the client has no prior awareness of the relevant problem and will vehemently reject the assessor's interpretation. This is actually an example of faulty empathy; an assessor mistakes a piece of level 1 or level 2 information for level 3 information. Typically this error occurs because the assessor is anxious about discussing some problem that is socially undesirable and does not want to embarrass the client or trigger the client's (and probably, the assessor's own) shame. It's as if some part of the assessor is anxiously asking, "How can I possibly tell someone that she has a thought disorder?" or "I can't tell this client that he is paranoid!" This anxiety then leads the assessor to avoid the relevant test finding by deciding, "This result is too far from the client's awareness to ever bring it up."

There are a number of things you should remember when this reaction arises. First, even if a problem shown on the MMPI-2 is one about which the client feels shame, you may greatly help the client by bringing the issue out into the light of day where it may be addressed in a compassionate, nonjudgmental manner. Second, many clients feel relief when you raise a topic they themselves have not been able to introduce. I still remember the first time I, with great anxiety and embarrassment, told a client that the MMPI suggested his thinking was idiosyncratic and bizarre. He sighed with great relief, and said "At last, someone has heard me! I've been wanting to talk about my strange thoughts for ages." Last, remember that clients often have a good sense of what they have revealed on the MMPI-2. If you fail to raise an issue which a client has reported in the test items, the client may jump to any of three

possible conclusions: the test is faulty, you are inept, or this
particular problem is too shameful to discuss openly.

Pause and Support the Client's Affective Reactions

During MMPI-2 feedback sessions clients often have strong
emotional reactions: sadness, anger, relief, joy, shame, or
fear. In most cases, such reactions are part of the therapeutic
process of the assessment, and you need do no more than stop
and encourage the client to notice and talk about her/his feelings, listen intently, and then support the client in accepting
or understanding her/his reactions. Such moments temporari-
ly interrupt your reporting of test findings to the client, but it
is important not to rush past the client's feelings. Supporting
the client's affective responses always takes precedence over
reporting more test findings; otherwise, the client will not be
able to integrate further findings and probably will get overwhelmed. Some clients are caught off guard by their strong
emotional reactions to feedback and try to stifle such reactions by urging you to go on. In such instances, you should
politely decline and quietly wait until the client can discuss
what she/he is feeling. Sometimes it helps to say something
encouraging like, "Oh that's okay. We're in no rush. A lot of
people have strong reactions to their test results. Can you tell
me some about what you're feeling and thinking?" After
clients have a chance to talk about a feeling and get support,
they will often signal that they are ready to proceed. Then you
may proceed with the next finding.

Closing the Feedback Session

The termination process in the MMPI-2 intervention typically
involves the last 5-10 minutes of the feedback session. This
too is an extremely important part of the assessment. As any
good clinician knows, engaging in a good termination with a
client increases the chance that an intervention will have a
lasting impact. This maxim is true even in the case of an
MMPI-2 assessment. Although the intervention is brief, it is

often an intense experience for the client, requiring a thoughtful termination. There are five recommended steps in closing the session:

1. Ask if the client has any questions. Some clients will pose entirely new questions to be answered by the testing at this point. This is especially likely if the client was skeptical about the assessment process initially but has felt confirmed and understood during the feedback session. Most clients will ask no questions at all or ask clarifying questions about findings that have already been discussed.

2. Check for distortions. This step is not necessary for all clients. However, if the MMPI-2 suggests a high probability of the client distorting the test feedback, or if you have grown concerned about possible distortions during the feedback session, ask the client to briefly summarize what was heard during the session. You can then confirm mutual understandings that developed in the session (findings with agreed-upon modifications) and raise any disagreements for further discussion.

3. Give permission for further contact. I always give permission for clients to contact me (directly or through their referring professionals) should further questions arise about the feedback session. I believe that by making this offer, I extend the supportive "holding environment" available to clients after the feedback session, when they are struggling to incorporate new understandings of themselves into their self-concepts.

4. Say good-bye. Assessors who are beginning to use the therapeutic assessment model are often astonished at how difficult it is to say good-bye to a client after an assessment intervention.[9] Often both assessor and client feel a great deal of sadness in parting and a longing to maintain contact in some way. Such feelings are partly a tribute to the depth of interpersonal connection client and assessor reached during the

---

[9] Obviously, if the assessor will continue to have professional contact with the client, this good-bye is not as final. However, it is still advisable for the assessor and client to say good-bye to the **assessment** relationship and discuss how the post-assessment relationship will be different.

assessment. I feel it is important for assessors to acknowledge feelings of connection and sadness openly, while simultaneously maintaining clear, appropriate boundaries for post-assessment contact with clients. In this way, the assessor models one of life's important lessons: that interpersonal connection and vulnerability are inextricably tied to grief, but grief need not be destructive when you can talk about it. By clearly saying good-bye, assessors also communicate their confidence that clients will take the understanding they reached during the assessment and apply it in their lives in their own ways.

For me a good-bye typically involves asking the client to share summary feedback or feelings about the entire assessment experience. If a client expresses gratitude for my part in the assessment I listen carefully and say "you're welcome." I then attempt to match the client's vulnerability by sharing something that I learned, or some personal experience I value from the assessment.

Post-Session Check-In

I recommend that you spend time immediately after a feedback session reflecting on several things:

Containment

My colleagues and I have found that "not telling everything" can be one of the most difficult aspects of a well-conducted feedback session. You will find that you often leave a feedback session with many unreported findings, either because they were in no way related to the client's assessment questions, or because a client proved unable to discuss a finding during the feedback session. This situation can be frustrating, and you must contain or deal with such frustration (and the unreported findings). If you do not consciously address the discomfort of containment, you may slowly drift away from doing assessments, or find yourself reporting too many test findings or findings that clients in no way invited or are ready to hear.

Containment is much less of a struggle when there is a referring professional involved with the assessment who can help
"hold" the information that couldn't be told the client. The
assessor then also knows that the unreported information
may find its way into the client's treatment at some later date.
When the client is self-referred, I sometimes find it useful to
have an imaginary conversation after the feedback session on
the topic of "what else the MMPI-2 suggested, but you didn't
seem ready to hear." Or I may speak confidentially with a
colleague about the MMPI-2 and the feedback session. At
other times, simply acknowledging my inner tension to myself
is enough for me contain it. Last, I find that as I practice containing, my "container" grows and I feel less and less tension
about not telling clients everything I know from their MMPI-2
profiles.

New lessons

After an assessment is completed (usually after the feedback
session), I often write a bit about "What I learned from this
assessment." I find it helpful to divide my lessons into three
categories:

➤ **What I learned about the MMPI-2.** Often, when
   reflecting on findings that the client confirmed, modified, or rejected, I find that the MMPI-2 profile fits better what the client said than does my own interpretation. By noting this, I continue to hone my skills in
   interpreting MMPI-2 code types and relative scale elevations.

➤ **What I learned about the client.** I may also discover
   things about the client that were not revealed by the
   MMPI-2 profile or the initial interview, and which
   have important implications for treatment planning.
   Here I consolidate my understanding of the client and
   expand my ability to put myself "in the client's shoes."

➤ **What I learned about myself.** If I have failed to inter-
   pret some portion of the MMPI-2 correctly, I may discover a blind spot in me to be explored later. Or I may

learn something about myself by reflecting on my emotional responses during the feedback session. Last, I often learn things about myself from clients' direct feedback about my part in an assessment.

By recording these three areas of learning, I help make future MMPI-2 assessments better for clients and myself.

The major steps in the MMPI-2 feedback session are summarized in Table 7.

Table 7

The Feedback Session

Set the client at ease by discussing any feelings about the feedback session

Remind the client of the assessment questions and solicit any additions

Frame the MMPI-2 as a communication from the client

Explain that the client will be asked to verify findings

Orient the client to the MMPI-2 profile

Answer the client's assessment questions using the MMPI-2 findings
- Begin with something positive
- Don't tell everything; select findings carefully
- Begin with findings the client will accept and gradually move to findings that challenge the client's current self-concept
- Tailor your language to the particular client

After each finding, enlist the client in verifying or modifying test findings

Never argue with a client about a test finding

Do not omit a test finding simply because it seems embarrassing to discuss

Pause and support the client's affective reactions as they occur

Close the feedback session
- Check for distortions in what the client heard/understood
- Give permission for the client to contact you in the future
- Say good-bye

Check-in with yourself after the feedback session
- What are you containing?
- What did you learn?

Special Issues Concerning Feedback Sessions

Involving a referring professional in the feedback session

If another professional has referred the client for the MMPI-2 assessment, it is quite useful to invite that colleague to attend the client feedback session. (Most referring professionals like to be present.) This arrangement ensures that the referring professional knows exactly what you have told the client about the test findings, should the client have questions or distort findings later on. Typically, this format also provides the client with additional emotional support during the feedback session.

It is generally a good idea to share the MMPI-2 findings with the referring professional before the client feedback session. Then you can focus exclusively on the client during the feedback session, rather than having to divide your attention between the client and the referring professional. Also, you may find it useful to consult with the referring professional about how to address the client during the feedback session—getting the referrer's sense of what findings the client will accept or reject and how the findings might best be worded for the client. Besides providing useful information, such consultation involves referring professionals as collaborators in the assessment process, helping them to feel included and important to the assessment.

Before the feedback session I typically share my sense of how the referring professional can be useful: by supporting the client's emotional reactions to feedback, coming up with examples that fit the test findings should the client have trouble making such connections, and spending some time with the client after the feedback session is over. As mentioned earlier, when the referring professional is present, the assessor can also take more risks in presenting potentially upsetting findings to the client.

There are other complexities to involving referring professionals in an assessment, especially, as often occurs, when the assessment referral is prompted by some breach in the relationship between the client and the referring professional.

Such issues are discussed in detail in Finn and Tonsager (in preparation).

When a client asks for a copy of the MMPI-2 profile

Some clients do this at the end of the feedback session, and it is worth exploring the request with a client before giving a copy of the profile or simply refusing to do so. Most often, a request for a copy of the profile stems from the client's wish to have something to hang onto after the assessment. I now anticipate such requests before they occur and encourage the client at the initial interview to bring a tape recorder to record the feedback session. Yet another solution, providing the client with a brief written test report, is discussed in more detail in the last section.

Very occasionally, a copy of the MMPI-2 profile is requested because clients feel skeptical about the assessor's test interpretation and wish to seek a second opinion from another professional. If this happens, it is best to try to discuss the clients' feelings further, while acknowledging their right to consult another professional. I then say that I prefer to give the actual MMPI-2 scores and graphs to an allied professional working with the client, explaining that all the graphs may not be very meaningful to the client and I fear that some scale names might be misleading.

There is a difference in opinion about what an assessor should do if a client still insists on having a full copy of the MMPI-2. Butcher (1990) recommends that one never consent to such a request. In Texas, state law is such that clients have legal access to all medical and mental-health records. If you are faced with such a request, it is best to consult with colleagues and attorneys in your particular area.

Adolescents

Although this manual has principally described an MMPI-2 intervention with adults, the procedures may easily be modified for using the MMPI-A with adolescents. I suggest several changes in how feedback sessions are arranged: typically I offer to give adolescents their own test feedback session before I talk with their parents about the assessment results. I then let them choose whether to attend the session I have with their parents. If they do plan to attend the joint session, I explain that mainly I will be addressing their parents but would welcome their chiming in with examples, agreements, or disagreements while I talk. I also make a special effort to represent their earlier reactions to a test finding (including any modifications) when discussing it with their parents. All of these steps help the adolescent client feel respected and included in the assessment process, and decrease any risk that I will be triangulated between the adolescent and the parents in the assessment.

Couples

Likewise, couples should be offered the chance to receive test feedback individually, before findings are presented in a joint session to both partners. After you review the individual MMPI-2 profiles in a joint session, it is often useful to discuss how the traits and problems of both partners are similar and dissimilar. Dorr (1981) has written about providing test feedback to clients during conjoint therapy.

Invalid defensive profiles

When the collaborative model is used with clients who voluntarily seek or assent to psychological testing, it is rare that an MMPI-2 profile is invalid owing to elevations on scales L and K. Should this occur, the collaborative assessor will not take the client's response as a personal affront, or lament the lack of "usable" test data. In fact, the validity scale elevations are themselves the major test findings, and they often shed light on the client's questions for the assessment. It is always good to bring humility to a feedback session with such clients, remembering that even your best efforts did not enlist the client's trust to either complete the MMPI-2 non-defensively or openly state her/his remaining reservations about the assessment. I have had valuable and enlightening discussions with such clients about how they find the whole idea of assessment untenable. Often I learned something about their situation that I had not previously understood.

Excerpts from Ms. C's Feedback Session

Initial moments

Ms. C arrived for her MMPI-2 feedback session wearing a slinky black dress, black stockings and high heels, and bright red lipstick—an outfit that struck me as both somewhat alluring and ominous—and raised my own anxiety. (I remember thinking, "She's dressed for war today.") Ms. C seemed aloof and slightly uninterested as she settled herself on the couch in my office and turned to face me. As I sat with my own anxiety, I realized that her attire and studied nonchalance probably reflected her anxiety about the feedback session. I then felt calmer and decided to address this anxiety openly:

SF: *"So what's it like coming in today to hear the results of the MMPI-2?"*

Ms. C: (shrugs her shoulders) *"No big deal. I still think the whole thing is ridiculous anyway, so it's not like I've been worrying about it."*

SF: *"What is it that seems ridiculous?"*

Ms. C: *"The thought that some test could tell me anything about myself that I don't already know."*

SF: *"That seems pretty far-fetched."*

Ms. C: (nodding head) *"Uh huh."*

SF: *"Well I can see how it would be hard to believe—especially if it seems that you already know yourself pretty well. Is that how you feel?"*

Ms. C: *"Yep. I've had a lot of time to think about myself and I really understand myself. What can anybody else tell me?"*

SF: *"Well, I guess we'll just have to see . . . (pause) . . . Are you still interested in hearing what the MMPI-2 said*

*about those questions you came up with the last time
we met?"*

Ms. C: *"I guess so. I already took it, so I might as well hear
what it says."*

SF: *"Okay, that's what we'll do today—look at those questions and the MMPI's answers. By the way, what was it
like taking the test?"*

At this point, Ms. C and I spoke a bit about her experience
taking the MMPI-2. (She complained about the "dumb" questions.) After that I reviewed the questions for the assessment,
although in a different order from which they were posed:

From Ms. Gomez:

1.   *Is Ms. C a good candidate for psychotherapy?*

From Ms. C:

2.   *Am I a danger to society?*

3.   *If I start drinking after probation, will it cause me problems?*

4.   *Am I manipulative?*

5.   *Why do I never seem to get along with men?*

This ordering reflected my attempt to gradually move from
level 1 to level 3 information in the feedback session. (See p.
51.) After restating the questions, I asked Ms. C if she had
any other questions to add. She did not, and so I oriented Ms.
C to the MMPI-2, using statements much like those presented
earlier, on pp. 49-50. Ms. C seemed to easily follow the explanation and no longer appeared nonchalant about the MMPI-
2. (She sat upright, eagerly following my finger as I pointed
out the different T-score levels.)

Test findings

I used the end of the MMPI-2 orientation to introduce a positive test finding and an acknowledgment that the test was a communication for Ms. C to me and Ms. Gomez:

SF: *"These scales over here are not problem scales like the others. They are designed to look at people's approach to taking the test . . .* (orientation to validity scales). *The first thing I want to tell you about your MMPI-2 results is that they say that you took the test seriously and answered the items carefully. It seems that you told the truth about yourself and weren't trying to make yourself look good or look bad. Is that your sense of things?"*

Ms. C: *"Absolutely. I'm glad the test shows that."*

SF: *"Well it does. I also want to thank you for your openness on the test. It makes my job interpreting it a lot easier and means we can take the scores on the problem scales seriously, without having to adjust for any distortions. I also really appreciate your approach to the test because I'm aware that you were kind of skeptical of the whole thing initially and that you even had a bad experience with assessment once."*

Ms. C: *"Well I figured if I were going to take it I might as well do it right, and you did promise you would tell me about the results if I wanted, even if you had to chase me down to find me."*

At this point I felt that Ms. C and I were ready to proceed with discussing the other, potentially more disturbing findings of the MMPI-2; she was clearly less anxious (as was I), and I felt that we had re-established the collaborative atmosphere achieved during the initial interview.

I first addressed the question from Ms. Gomez, believing that my answer would help Ms. C view me as an ally in her struggle to maintain some control over her life while on probation:

SF: (having repeated the question) *"I can't point to any particular scale to answer this first question, but the overall pattern of your MMPI-2 results suggests that individual psychotherapy probably wouldn't be very useful to you right now. It doesn't look like you're in a lot of distress or that you're the type of person to turn to others for help. I just can't see why you'd want to be in therapy right now, and therapy isn't usually very successful unless a person wants to be there. Does that seem right to you?"*

Ms. C: *"That's exactly what I've been trying to tell Ms. Gomez—that I don't want or need it right now. Better they should use the money to send someone who wants to be in therapy. I don't!"*

SF: *"Well that fits with the MMPI. So I'll say exactly that to Ms. Gomez, that individual therapy isn't likely to help right now. Now sometimes people with scores like yours do benefit from being in a group. What would you think of that?"*

Ms. C: *"The same thing. I don't want to right now. If I need help in the future I might consider it. But I probably wouldn't because everything you say just gets reported back to the Probation Department."*

SF: *"Is that how it works when you're on probation?"*

Ms. C: *"Yep. If they really wanted to help people they would have groups that would be confidential."*

SF: *"Perhaps I'll say that to Ms. Gomez too, just in case you ever want to go to a group in the future."*

This interaction seemed very successful to me and thus I decided to proceed with the next question, "Am I a danger to society?" Again, I kept mainly to level 1 information.

SF: *"Let me show you the MMPI scale that I think relates most to this question (pointing to Scale 4). This is a scale that has to do with anger and rebelliousness. As you can see, you scored high on this scale, meaning that you endorsed a lot of items about anger and rebelliousness. Your scores suggest that you are especially angry at authority figures and are likely to do the opposite of what they tell you to do. People with scores like yours often let their anger out by breaking lots of rules; they have run-ins with the cops, use drugs and alcohol to excess, and like to do things that are risky and exciting. (Pause—watching Ms. C's face.) Does that fit with how you see yourself?"*

Ms. C: *"Yeah, I like all those things. But does that mean I'm a menace to society?"*

SF: *"Well there's where I'm not sure I understand what that counselor meant. The MMPI-2 would say that you're real angry, and that you can easily do some things that are dangerous to yourself or people around you, but I don't see that as being the same as a walking menace or a 'danger to society.'"*

Ms. C: *"That's what I think. I know I do some stupid things sometimes, but it's not like I'm a monster or something."*

SF: *"I agree. What kinds of stupid things do you do when you're angry?"*

Ms. C: *"Oh like go on a drinking binge, except I can't do that now. Or get into a big fight with some friend. Or the prank that got me on probation."*

SF: *"Those things fit with the MMPI. Have you ever been in trouble with the law before this recent time?"*

Ms. C: *"Not really. I almost had some trouble once as a teenager. I got caught shoplifting. But my parents worked it out with the store that I had to pay for what I took. That was close."*

SF: *"How about doing things that are dangerous to you? The MMPI-2 would say you might do some pretty risky things."*

Ms. C: *"Well I guess I've been that way about sex. It used to be I would get in some scary situations by going home with men I didn't even know. But I haven't been doing that lately either."*

SF: *"That kind of sexual behavior is another thing that goes along with this scale on the MMPI-2"* (points to Scale 4).

Notice that the key to the successful interaction around this question was that I answered both the overt question (Can I be dangerous?) and the underlying question (Am I a monster?). I also accepted a modification of my test interpretation; Ms. C didn't appear to have as great a history of flagrant acting out as one might have expected from the MMPI-2.

There was an easy transition from the above question to Question 3 ("If I start drinking after probation, will it cause me problems?"). I strongly stressed the likelihood of alcohol contributing to Ms. C's acting-out behavior, and the association of the spike 4 and 4-8 code types to alcohol abuse. Ms. C did not seem at all surprised by my statements and confirmed that she herself knew that drinking was probably associated with a number of her problems. An important event in this section of the feedback session was that Ms. C expressed some sadness about having to give up alcohol, and I was able to emotionally support her:

Ms. C: *"I just hate hearing that* [I'm at risk of more troubles if I continue drinking] *even though I think the test is probably right."*

SF: *"What's the hardest thing about hearing that you probably shouldn't be drinking at all?"*

Ms. C: *"It's always been a part of me. I mean I'm not drinking right now because of the urine tests, but if I think I can never drink again I have to invent a whole new me."*

SF: *"Which must mean saying good-bye to the old you."*

Ms. C: *"Yes, that's what this is all about. I'm not fifteen any-more with no responsibilities and able to get drunk every night. I'm twenty-four and I have to watch out for myself now. But I wish I could be fifteen and carefree again."*

SF: *"The drinking was part of the old irresponsible you, and now you're trying to be more responsible and stay out of trouble."*

Ms. C: *"That's right and I hate having to give the old me up."*

At this point in the session (30 minutes in), I felt a deep empathic connection to Ms. C. I sensed the troubled young girl underneath the vamp exterior that she showed, and I could feel the sadness of losing part of an old identity—an experience that I had recently gone through myself. Ms. C and I sat in silence for several minutes. Then I gradually brought us back to the remaining assessment questions:

SF: *"Do you feel ready to go on to another question?"*

Ms. C: *"Yes"*

SF: *"Then let me talk about this next one: 'Am I manipulative?'"*

Ms. C: *"Okay."*

SF: *"People use that word to mean different things, so again I'm not sure what that counselor meant by saying you were manipulative. But there are a few scales on the MMPI that might pertain to this. This scale (pointing to Scale 3) has to do with wanting to be taken care of, and your score suggests that there is probably a part of you—just as in most of us—that wishes that somebody would come in and just take care of all your needs and problems. It might be related to that young part you mentioned, who just wants to be able to be irresponsi-ble. Does that seem right?"*

Ms. C: *"I guess so. Sometimes I would just like to turn my prob-lems over to someone else and not think about them."*

SF: *"Right. Well the MMPI-2 suggests that the part in you that wants to be taken care of is pretty strong, but it probably is directly in conflict with another part, who wants to be pretty independent and hates asking for things from other people. This scale here (Scale 6) has to do with not wanting to ask other people for things directly and suggests you really don't like doing that. Does that fit you?"*

Ms. C: *"Oh yes. I hate asking for anything. I'd rather do it all by myself."*

SF: *"Okay, so here's where manipulative comes in. I'm wondering if you haven't found some ways to try to get things from people—to satisfy that part of you that wants to be taken care of—but ways that would be indirect rather than direct. That way you wouldn't have to ask for things outright. And if so, I'm thinking this behavior is what the counselor might have called 'manipulative.'"*

Ms. C: *"Hmm . . . you mean I might try to get things I want without having to come right out and say it?"*

SF: *"Yes."*

Ms. C: *"Well I guess that's true. Would that be like me trying to dress nice so that men will pay attention to me?"*

SF: *"Maybe. Or even dressing nice so that you could get them to give you something or cut you some slack. Do you ever do that?"*

Ms. C: (smiling) *"Yeah, like in the alcohol treatment I guess I did try to be nice to this one counselor, so he'd give me a good evaluation. That's the one who called me 'manipulative.'"*

SF: *"Now that's exactly the kind of thing the MMPI-2 would predict. By the way, does all this have anything to do with the way you're dressed today?"*

Ms. C: *"Well sort of, but it's not exactly the same. I knew I couldn't change what the test said by how I dressed,*

> *but this outfit made me feel stronger this morning. I guess to tell the truth, I was kind of scared after all."*

SF: *"I understand, so you were just trying to feel better, not trying to get anything from me."*

Ms. C: *"That's right."*

SF: *"And how's the fear right now?"*

Ms. C: *"Much better."*

In the next section of the feedback session, Ms. C and I discussed her final assessment question ("Why do I never seem to get along with men?"). In answering this question, I focused first on findings that had already been presented (i.e., extreme anger, wanting to be taken care of but not being able to ask directly). I then ran into my first disagreement with Ms. C, when I attempted to suggest that underlying insecurity might lead her to choose men who were not her equals.

SF: *"Women with scores like yours often don't feel very good about themselves deep down. They're actually quite insecure. Therefore, they sometimes get together with men who don't have much to offer, so they won't feel scared of getting rejected. Then they get mad when the men disappoint them."*

Ms. C: (Pauses, while wrinkling her nose.) *"That doesn't seem right. I agree that I've been with a lot of losers. But I don't agree with the part about not feeling good about myself. Sure, I've got my faults like anybody, but I generally like myself okay."*

SF: *"I see. So do you have any ideas why you get hooked up with losers?"*

Ms. C: *"I don't know. I guess I'm just a slow learner. Or maybe because I was drunk all the time—it just took me a while to catch on."*

SF: *"So as far as you know, you don't feel insecure about your-self inside, or sometimes wonder if you're worthwhile?"*

Ms. C: *"Nope. Sorry. The test's done pretty good today. But that one's wrong."*

SF: *"Okay. I guess as you said, the test's done pretty good. So why don't I just stop here and see if you have any other questions?"*

As you can see, I judged that Ms. C had had enough for one day (and so perhaps had I), and thus I simply backed down without attempting any further discussion of low self-esteem. At this point, she had no more questions, so I showed her the brief report I had prepared, and invited her to comment on it, which she did. (See more about this in the following section.)

Closing

We then moved toward ending the session:

SF: *"So how do you feel about having gone through this?"*

Ms. C: *"Pretty good. I never thought a test could tell me any-thing about myself, but this one did. And except for that one thing about the insecurity, it was right on."*

SF: *"Well I'm glad that you thought so. What did you learn that was new for you?"*

Ms. C: *"Well I wasn't surprised about the doing dangerous things, or about the drinking being a problem. But I guess I never knew how angry I was, and that bit about being manipulative was all new."*

SF: *"So that was helpful for you."*

Ms. C: *"Yes, I guess I'll be thinking about that one for a while. So you'll send that report to Ms. Gomez?"*

SF: *"Yes, I'll put it in the mail today."*

Ms. C: (rolls eyes) *"So I guess we'll be talking about it when I*
           see her on Friday. Well thanks, this was really okay. I
           thought it was going to be awful."

SF: *"You're welcome, and thanks for talking with me about*
           what it's like to give up drinking. I've never understood
           before how that would seem like losing a part of yourself."

Table 8

Post-Assessment Reflections on Ms. C

Dear Ms. C,

You're an amazing woman! You came in so haughty and defended, I was afraid nothing I said would make sense to you. But you took almost everything in and gave back a lot too. I was so touched by that piece about losing your identity with the drinking. You were really vulnerable when you talked about that. I wish you'd been able to talk with me more about the underlying insecurity; I really feel there's some truth there that could help you. But I'm sure that idea was too much, and you had already stretched so far by the end.

What I learned about the MMPI-2
It seemed to overplay the acting-out in this case. Or perhaps I didn't weigh Scale 3 enough as an inhibitor variable. I'll have to do more reading about this or perhaps call Jim Butcher and ask him.

What I learned about Ms. C
When someone takes her side, she can let down her defenses fairly rapidly. I'll have to speak with Ms. Gomez and ask how she's dealing with her. There was a lot of vulnerability under the character armor that shows up on the MMPI-2. I wonder if projective testing would have shown that soft side, or whether she would have been too defended? I wonder if I was too pessimistic about therapy? If it's not part of a power struggle, and she didn't have to ask for it directly, might she go to therapy and benefit after all?

What I learned about myself
I'm getting better at managing my own anxiety so I can connect with clients. I did much better with Ms. C than with the last probation client. Even so, I was really anxious today at first. I wonder if it was the disdain or the seductiveness that bothered me more? I'll have to talk about that with K. And I really felt a response in me as she talked about losing her identity with the drinking. I guess it touches that part of me that still feels the loss of identity with my recent job change.

Ms. C: *"So that might help you with some other patient?"*

SF: *"Yes, I'm sure it will, and it touched me too."*

Ms. C: *"Cool. I taught the shrink something."*

Soon after that, we shook hands and Ms. C left, looking relaxed and confident. I immediately sat down and wrote out the notes shown in Table 8.

Written MMPI-2 Reports for Clients

Since the Finn and Tonsager (1992) study was completed, my colleagues and I have begun to routinely tape-record feedback sessions for clients and/or to write brief written reports for clients about their MMPI-2 results. Written reports basically answer clients' assessment questions and are tailored to individual clients, just as are oral feedback sessions. Thus the report for someone with a 2-7 code type is typically quite different from that written for a client with a 4-9 code type. Also, written reports obviously differ depending on the questions clients have posed for the assessment. Written MMPI-2 reports are discussed in Finn and Tonsager (in preparation). Also Fischer (1985) has written extensively about individualized psychological reports for clients. One of Fischer's collaborative strategies that we have adopted is to ask clients to write down their reactions to the assessment on the back of the report. Table 9 shows the written report for Ms. C, and her comments appear in Figure 3.

Table 9

Written Report Given to Ms. C and Her Response

MMPI-2 Report

Client: Ms. C   Date of report:
Age: 24   Referred by: Ms. Gomez

Summary of answers to assessment questions:

1. **Is Ms. C a good candidate for psychotherapy?** (From Ms. Gomez)
   The MMPI-2 suggests that Ms. C would have a lot of difficulties in individual psychotherapy. She really does not appear to be in enough distress to be motivated for therapy, she is not likely to trust a therapist easily, and she is not the type of person to openly ask others for help when she needs it. She might benefit from group therapy but, again, only if she were motivated to attend.

2. **Am I a danger to society?**
   The MMPI-2 suggests that you are extremely angry inside, especially at authority figures. Women with scores like yours often do things that are dangerous to themselves or others, but this does not mean that they can't learn to control such behavior. You'll decrease the chances of your doing dangerous things if you work on dealing with your anger directly.

3. **If I start drinking after probation, will it cause me problems?**
   Persons with test scores like yours often have a long history of run-ins with the law. They often do crazy things when they are drinking. You'll be most likely to stay out of trouble if you stay sober.

4. **Am I manipulative?**
   You may want people to take care of you, but are likely to avoid asking directly. You might ask in indirect ways that people see as "manipulative."

5. **Why do I never seem to get along with men?**
   The MMPI-2 suggests that your intense anger might make you come off as "bitchy" to men. You might expect men to give you what you want without your having to ask; if so, you'll always be disappointed and they'll feel unjustly accused.

   Women with scores like yours don't feel very good about themselves deep down. They tend to hook up with men who aren't their equals and then get angry when the men disappoint them.

Stephen E. Finn, Ph.D.
Licensed Psychologist

I expected this test to be worthless, but it wasn't. I do know some things about myself that didn't know before and it was pretty acurate.

I agree with every thing in the report except for not feeling good about myself deep down. I feel good about myself. I just keep hooking up with losers and I still don't know why.

Ms. Gomez, I hope you see he doesn't think I should go to therapy either

Figure 3. Ms. C's Comments on the MMPI-2 Report

Concluding Remarks

Typically the MMPI-2 has been viewed as an aid in planning therapeutic interventions that take place after an assessment, and little attention has been paid to the process by which clients are administered the test. This traditional outlook on the MMPI-2 (and on psychological assessment in general) ignores the interpersonal context of clients' test responses and promotes a mechanistic, de-humanized approach to psychological testing. Such an approach is sometimes harmful to clients and at best benefits them only indirectly. It is not surprising that many gifted clinicians have rejected the traditional use of psychological tests such as the MMPI-2 nor that currently many insurance companies are questioning the value of psychological assessment (Finn & Martin, in preparation).

In this manual I have attempted to spell out a collaborative, empathic approach to MMPI-2 test use, which is based on the assumption that an MMPI-2 assessment can have a significant therapeutic impact on clients. The extensive research base underlying MMPI-2 code-type interpretation, the rich inferences that can be drawn regarding personality and interpersonal relationships, and the sensitive validity scales all combine to make the MMPI-2 an ideal instrument for use in brief clinical interventions. Controlled research has demonstrated that clients are more hopeful, less distressed, and have higher self-esteem after receiving MMPI-2 feedback in the fashion described in this manual (Finn & Tonsager, 1992). Currently, my colleagues and I are conducting additional studies of the therapeutic power of the MMPI-2; we hope to identify additional ways to use the test in benefitting clients.

References

American Psychological Association. (1992). Ethical principles of psychologists and code of conduct. *American Psychologist*, 47, 1597-1628.

Butcher, J. N. (1990). *The MMPI-2 in psychological treatment.* New York: Oxford University Press.

Butcher, J. N., & Finn, S. E. (1983). Objective personality assessment in clinical settings. In M. Hersen, A. E. Kazdin, & A. S. Bellack (Eds.), *The clinical psychology handbook* (pp. 329-344). New York: Pergamon Press.

Butcher, J. N., Graham, J. R., Williams, C. L., & Ben-Porath, Y. S. (1990). *Development and use of the MMPI-2 Content Scales.* Minneapolis: University of Minnesota Press.

Butcher, J. N., & Williams, C. L. (1992). *Essentials of MMPI-2 and MMPI-A interpretation.* Minneapolis: University of Minnesota Press.

Erdberg, P. (1979). A systematic approach to providing feedback from the MMPI. In C. Newmark (Ed.), *MMPI clinical and research trends* (pp. 328-342). New York: Praeger.

Dorr, D. (1981). Conjoint psychological testing in marriage therapy: New wine in old skins. *Professional Psychology*, 12, 549-555.

Finn, S. E., & Butcher, J. N. (1991). Clinical objective personality assessment. In M. Hersen, A. E. Kazdin, & A. S. Bellack (Eds.), *The clinical psychology handbook* (2nd ed.; pp. 362-373). New York: Pergamon Press.

Finn, S. E., & Martin, H. (in preparation). Therapeutic assessment with the MMPI-2 in managed health care. In J. N. Butcher (Ed.), *Treatment planning with the MMPI-2 in a managed-care environment.*

Finn, S. E., & Tonsager, M. E. (1992). Therapeutic effects of providing MMPI-2 test feedback to college students awaiting psychotherapy. *Psychological Assessment, 3,* 278-287.

Finn, S. E., & Tonsager, M. E. (in preparation). *Therapeutic assessment: Using psychological testing to help clients change.*

Fischer, C. T. (1985/1994). *Individualizing psychological assessment.* Hillsdale, NJ: Lawrence Erlbaum.

Graham, J. R. (1993). *MMPI-2: Assessing personality and psychopathology,* 2nd edition. New York: Oxford University Press.

Greene, R. (1991). *The MMPI-2/MMPI: An interpretive manual.* Boston: Allyn and Bacon.

Lewak, R. W., Marks, P. A., & Nelson, G. E. (1990). *Therapist guide to the MMPI & MMPI-2.* Muncie, Indiana: Accelerated Development, Inc.

Webb, J. T., & McNamara, K. M. (1978). *Configural interpretation of the MMPI.* Columbus, OH: Ohio Psychology Publishing.